STRUCTURE AND GUTS OF CHARACTER EDUCATION

A MORAL COMPASS FOR EDUCATORS

**Structure and Guts of Character Education:
A Moral Compass for Educators**
by David Streight

No part of this book may be used or reproduced in any manner without written permission, except in the case of brief quotations embodied in critical articles or reviews. For information or permissions, contact CSEE.

Copies of this and other CSEE publications are available through the Center for Spiritual and Ethical Education

Purchase information at
- www.csee.org
- 800.298.4599
- info@csee.org

Discounts available for school purchases of 10 or more copies.

© 2015 by David Streight and CSEE

ISBN: 978-1-881678-85-4

To
Marie-Claire

*a committed, genuine professional
who doesn't flaunt it
probably doesn't even think it;
of that, I often stand in awe*

Table of Contents

Chapter 1: The Structure of Character Education	7
Chapter 2: The Lens of Well-Being	9
Chapter 3: Identifying Goals	23
Chapter 4: Packaged Programs	37
Chapter 5: Permeation	43
Chapter 6: Assessment	59
Chapter 7: The Guts of Character Education	69
Chapter 8: Autonomy	73
Chapter 9: Relatedness	91
Chapter 10: Competence	99
Chapter 11: Praise, Criticism, & Feedback	107
Chapter 12: On Purpose	117
References	123

1

The Structure of Character Education

Over the course of a decade working on "character" with educators, the realization has dawned on this writer that many schools would be better positioned for success in their character development initiatives if they had more clarity in two areas. The first is basic process, including consensus on what they want to accomplish and a roadmap to reach their destination. The second is clarity on how to maximize the chances that their work will lead not just to positive growth, but to enduring and intrinsically motivated growth in students.

These two areas point to the two sections of this book. The first has to do with structuring a program for character development. I have not seen others speak exactly in terms of the paradigm offered here, though I do believe that character experts all agree completely with the elements the paradigm outlines: the need for goals that people at school understand and agree on; coordinated efforts to imbue all aspects of school life with those goals; and some intentional effort to check to see if those coordinated efforts are having success. These elements constitute what this book is calling the Structure; in shorthand, it's goals, permeation, and assessment. In no way do these three elements of "structure" imply that goals, permeation, and assessment are all that is needed; but the three elements are essential to a program that is responsible, and effective.

The second section of the book deals with the Guts, which really is where the "heart" of character development resides. It is possible to have all the structure in place—clear goals, a wide range of individuals and programs working to make those goals a reality, and careful inquiry into how all is working, but structure is the outside work. Character development—the kind educators want—happens on the inside. It cannot be pushed in, even by benevolent outsiders. Behavior can be manipulated, coerced, even enticed, but behavior and character are not the same thing.

The change educators really aspire to is inner change—not pushed in from the outside, but rather brought in from the inside and integrated into the self because of its value, because it feels right. This distinction between behavior and character will arise at a number of points in the pages to come. Of course character educators want good behavior too, but their sights are set on inner development, on the kind of development that motivates consideration for the well-being of oneself and others.

The Guts part of this book, then, offers a practical summary of the best research currently available to educators regarding how to foster that inner development in students. It answers the question "What can educators do to maximize the possibility that students will develop into sensitive, considerate, caring human beings whose behavior comes not from outside demands, expectations, or enticements, but from the deepest inner motivation?"

The beauty of the Guts section lies in the now demonstrated wisdom it offers: practices in no way limited to members of the character education committee or a few other select individuals, but rather strategies and practices that can be employed by every adult who works with kids in a school (or in a family). The Guts of character development focuses primarily on three needs that all human beings must have filled if they are to lead healthy psychological and social lives: the need to feel a certain amount of control over one's life, to pursue the kind of life one values (autonomy); the need for warm and supportive relationships; and the need to feel like one has the skills (competence) needed to meet challenges normally faced in life.

2

The Lens of Well-Being

On the Purpose of Education

In the spring of 2014 we asked 200 independent school administrators to participate in a short survey. The main goal was to get a sense of what leaders in some of the finest schools in North America saw as the purpose of their profession. What resulted suggests that there is little consensus regarding why we are doing what we are doing in schools. Similar surveys since that time, with some 500 other educators, have offered the same conclusion.

The reason for recounting the results of these surveys is that what follows in this chapter is an argument for two kinds of clarity. The first is clarity in goals, especially regarding goals for character development, but character development goals should follow from goals for education in general. The second is a call for clarity in practice; specifically it is a call for educators to tailor practices in schools—meaning interactions, of all kinds, with students and peers—toward accomplishing the goals they want to meet. The quest for clarity is based in part on three premises, the first of which is this:

> *We have a better chance of reaching our goals*
> *if we know what our goals are.*

Few people disagree with the statement, and yet it is surprising that educators have so little agreement on (and sometimes so little sense of) what the main goal—the primary purpose—of their profession is. Many educators facing the question in workshops even need time to think before articulating an answer, as if they had not

thought about it since…who knows when? All their post-reflection responses are positive, of course. They include purpose-of-education statements like:
- to prepare young people today for the world's needs tomorrow
- to create lifelong learners
- to get kids ready for college and life
- to help students become independent thinkers and problem solvers
- to pass on the heritage of the past, and teach skills for the future

But the list goes on…Schools continue to "teach stuff" to kids, to begin new initiatives, and even to engage in new strategic plans; but does it not seem logical that those engaged in such endeavors should know what their school's goals are and then, in some way, aim their practice toward fulfillment of those goals? If each educator in a school has a different vision of why he or she is there, is it fair to argue that their collective effectiveness is in some way diminished?

> **Three Premises**
>
> 1. We have a better chance of reaching our goals if we know what our goals are.
>
> 2. We have a better chance of reaching our goals if we work together on them as a team.
>
> 3. We have a better chance of students being exemplars of our goals if they know what our goals are.

When the administrators responded to the second survey question, the pattern of answers was just as scattered, up to a certain point. The way the survey was constructed, half of the participants were asked for a description; this item asked them to think about the "typical talented graduate" of their school, and, in one sentence, to describe what they hoped he or she would be like 20 years after graduation. Once again, no prevalent description resulted. Responses addressed a smattering of accomplishments, talents, and virtues—all nice and good—but absolutely nothing to resemble a bell curve of consensus.

The curious thing about these surveys was how the pattern of results took shape when only one word was changed to make that second question more dynamic. The first half of survey takers were asked what they hoped their graduates would be *like* 20 years after graduation (italics were not used in the question). The other half of the survey takers were presented with the question "If your school is successful, what do you hope the typical talented graduate will be *doing* 20 years after graduation?" In contrast to the scattered blast of answers to the question asking for a description (What do you hope the graduate will be like…?), or to the question regarding the purpose of education, a remarkable consensus formed when the question was phrased to focus on how educators hoped graduates would be living their lives. Over three quarters of the responses to the "doing" question converged around two central, and quite complementary, ideas. The first was an other-directed desire for service or social responsibility, with a focus on positive change.

*What do you hope your talented alums will be **doing** 20 years after graduation?*

Specifically, three-fifths (62%) of the respondents hoped that their graduates would be doing something to meet the needs of others. Their statements included phrases like "improving the lives of others," "doing service of some kind," "contributing to the world's needs," or simply "helping others." Answers as ambiguous as "being a responsible citizen" were not included in this 62%, by the way, because despite the fact that being a good citizen is desirable, it is possible to interpret it as doing the minimum expected, as keeping the sum at zero, so to speak. Being a responsible citizen, for example, could conceivably describe someone who pays the required taxes, stays out of trouble, and keeps his lawn mowed, but nothing more. On the other hand, doing service, like the other answers included in this overwhelmingly large set of responses, is not a requirement of citizenship, it is supererogatory, extra; it concerns working above and beyond the minimum on behalf of one's fellow human beings. So many respondents; such disparate articulations; yet such common hope for the future!

The second large category of answers was more inner-focused. Respondents wanted graduates to tap into what gave them personal meaning, into what fed their individual passions. These replies—offered by fully half of the respondents—wanted graduates to find meaning and purpose in their lives, sometimes stated as discovering, and acting in accord with, where their unique passions lie, or what most fulfills them. The implication is that each of our students has a specific, yet very individual and personal set of talents and interests that, if discerned, unlocks the door to a certain "meaningful rightness" in life. Responses as ambiguous as "doing something they like" or as bland as "living a good life" or "having a good job" (which some administrators did offer), were not included in the 50%, because they stood qualitatively apart from answers where it was possible to see meaning, purpose, or passion. For example, some respondents might consider "a good life" to be one with plenty of money and a high level of status or comfort. The 50% of responses included in the second category, on the other hand, used phrases that suggested a meaningful, personally relevant aim, like "finding their purpose in life" or "working in the area of their passion."

It all points to the fullest possible development of personally-discerned potential, and dedication to the well-being of others.

Moreover, over a quarter of all respondents (28%) included both helping others and meaning/passion in their responses. In other words, when asked what they hoped their talented graduates would be doing twenty years after graduation, they offered replies like:

- Actualizing their gifts and passions for the good of all, ideally for the betterment of all.
- Doing work where his or her passions meet the world's needs.
- Pursuing her passions and dreams and helping contribute to the creation of a more equitable world.

Such responses to this same question had occurred in even higher percentages in a workshop a few weeks earlier, where 90% of the "doing" answers reflected either one or both of the two response categories covering social service and purpose or passion. We've done the same exercise on other occasions where the numbers were not as high, and yet without exception the pattern of responses has been exactly the same: when educators were asked to answer in one sentence what they hope their fine alums will be doing two decades after school, the number one answer concerned work to improve the lives of others. In their second most common asnwer, they hoped graduates would discern personal purpose, passion, or meaning, and then be able to act on it. Though the sampling of respondents for these surveys was overwhelmingly from private independent schools, the consistency of responses from one group to the next, and the way they bunched around the same two concepts, in the same order, invites serious consideration.

Two things seem to follow from this. The first suggests that even if they have a hard time articulating a common purpose, a large number of educators agree on the kind of world they want as a result of their professional efforts: they want a world where their students are engaged in meeting the needs of, and advancing the quality of life for, those around them. Moreover, they seem to feel this engagement happens best when those involved in creating a better world are doing so out of what feeds a personal sense of purpose, when they are acting out of their own sense of a meaningful and passionately-lived life. It all points to the fullest possible development of personally-discerned potential, and dedication to the well-being of others.

The second implication is more troubling, though, given the disparity between the purpose statements and the "doing" statements of many. It is as if these educators are conflicted, saying "I think the purpose of education is x, but I hope my school will produce kids who are y and z." Ideally, the x, the y, and the z should all line up; if we take a little time to get clarity of purpose, it should not be difficult to align, and articulate, a route from x to z. We really only know what our goals are if we are able to articulate them. In the classroom, what we teach and how we teach should be influenced by why we teach. And why we teach—what our ultimate, most deeply held goal is—needs to be kept in the forefront of our efforts.

The consensus of these educators' statements seems to come down to this statement: the purpose of education is to foster in students the skills, and the will, to realize their own personally meaningful potential for nurturing well-being in themselves and in the wider community.

Because well-being—a concept to be revisited shortly—is inextricably interwoven with one's sense of personal purpose, this statement might be shortened even more:

the purpose of education is to foster in students the skills, and the will, to nurture their own well-being and that of the wider community.

An understanding of the term *well-being* will help connect the dots between this statement and what the educators said.

Why frame the goal in terms of well-being, as opposed to formulations like creating lifelong learners, preparing young people to be contributing members of society, teaching students the skills to solve the problems of tomorrow's world? All these ideas are good, but they stop short of the ideal destination. Lifelong learning, for example, is but one important detail in an incomplete picture. Do we care what lifelong learning entails, or is our more central concern that young people's continued learning help them be better equipped to contribute meaningfully to society?

The large preponderance of all the purpose statements from the surveys mentioned above (to prepare young people today for the world's needs tomorrow, creating lifelong learners, preparation for college…) are congruent with the purpose statement focusing on well-being, even as they stop short of it. Having a successful college career is something we would want for nearly all our students; the skills of critical inquiry and an appreciation of artistic beauty certainly can contribute to the attainment of well-being. The same is true in regard to career preparation. A life of well-being is difficult without work that is meaningful, work that pays acceptably well, and work that brings a certain sense of satisfaction and success. Preparing young people to be participants in democracy similarly envisions an endpoint of a well-functioning society. But the ultimate purpose of a well-working democracy, of a great society, is precisely that of establishing the social, psychological, and economic conditions that allow its members to flourish, is it not?

Each school needs to come to its own agreement on the purpose of education. The purpose statement above is an opinion neither carved in stone nor written in the sky. But before moving too much further, the reader should have some clarity regarding his or her own idea either of the profession's purpose, or at least of what the ultimate goal of "character development" should be.

Structure & Guts of Character Education

Clarifying well-being and flourishing

Popular culture uses *well-being* in relatively nondescript ways, but the term has taken on a more specific meaning as researchers, organizations, and governments realize its intrinsic value. Well-being in the context of this chapter refers not just to the sense of being happy or "well off" (Clark & Senik, 2011), or as used by Diener (2015) and others; nor does it refer to a life of pleasure or one simply filled with positive emotions. The term refers rather to a life—and to the way it is lived—that is characterized not just by a deep sense of satisfaction, but also of rightness. The rightness and satisfaction result from the realization that, with a combination of one's own capacities and certain environmental supports, one is growing into what Alan Waterman refers to as one's own "personally significant potentialities" (1990, p. 41). Over the past twenty-five years, but increasingly just in the past decade, a set of characteristics with significant overlap has been identified. Veronika Huta and Alan Waterman (2013) recently constructed a chart as they attempted to bring some unity to, and set new directions for, this important field. The list of factors contributing to well-being outlined below comes from years of work by psychologist Carol Ryff (1989; Ryff & Keyes, 1995), who was studying well-being earlier than many individuals better known today, and who has offered probably the strongest research-based argument for the components.

Think about each of Ryff's factors for well-being from the perspective of its appropriateness as a characteristic of the ideal alum of your school 20 years after graduation. Or better yet, think about their desirability for a student sitting in class today:

self acceptance
She feels generally positive about herself, about her skills, her talents, and her life, even while she acknowledges and accepts that some of her skills and talents are better and some are weaker than others.

relationships
She understands the give and take of human relationships; she has warm, satisfying, and trusting relationships with others; she cares about the welfare of others; she is capable of empathy, affection and intimacy.

autonomy
She feels she has a fair amount of control over her life; she is an independent thinker, able to resist outside pressures to form opinions or act in certain ways; her behavior is self-regulated; she evaluates herself according to internal, self-determined standards rather than the standards of peers or the media.

environmental mastery
She feels she has the skills to meet most of the challenges that life and situations will present; she makes effective use of opportunities that arise; she knows how to choose and take advantage of options that meet her needs and values.

purpose in life
She feels that her life has meaning; she has discerned goals to accomplish in life and has a sense of direction toward which she is working.

personal growth
The successes she has experienced give her the sense that she is continuing to grow as a person; she is open to new experiences, and has a sense of being on a path toward realizing her personal potential; she is growing in ways that reflect greater self-knowledge and increased effectiveness (Ryff, 1989).

What ties these six factors together is their research base for laying the foundations for the development of personal potential, the foundations for growing into the person one feels one can and should become (Ryff, 1989; Ryff & Keyes, 1995). Individuals characterized by these descriptors both report a deeper satisfaction with life and are seen by themselves and others to be functioning more fully, both socially and emotionally, and by virtue of this they are able to engage in more mature moral action than would otherwise be the case. The well-being that results from a critical mass of the six is close to the end goal that, it seems, most purpose-of-education statements start to focus on, but do not quite reach. Why "lifelong learners," for example, if not lifelong learners of what is needed to live a flourishing life, meaning a long life of assimilating the information and skills involved in forming and maintaining trusting and supportive relationships, in thinking and acting independent of outside pressures, in working to accomplish purpose-defined goals, and in continuing to grow as a person? Or why "prepare kids for college and life" if not in hopes that college will prepare them for a life that flourishes because it is full of meaning? Or why "prepare people today for the world's needs tomorrow," unless we are laying the foundations for a world that makes such well-being possible?

A number of governmental organizations have begun to consider that well-being is ultimately a better measure of political success and responsible governance than measures—like the GDP in the United States—of how much a population consumes, or how much money a population spends. The United Kingdom now has an Office of National Statistics with a "Measuring National Well-Being Programme" that keeps track of "how the UK as a whole is doing" (Randall & Corp, 2014). Since 2003, 28 nations in Europe have been participating every four years in a European Quality of Life Survey that assesses life satisfaction and happiness, among other things (Clark & Senik, 2011; Huppert & So, 2009); and the tiny nation of Bhutan is now famous for its decision to make Gross National Happiness the focal point of its domestic policy. Ed Diener, a psychologist at the University of Illinois at Urbana-Champaign, recently published a list of 43 nations in which "a governmental or international agency has collected measures of subjective well-being" (Diener, 2015, p. 235). Despite Derek Bok's *The Politics of Happiness* (2010) and the decade of work by the European nations, Australia, and others, the United States is behind the well-being curve; but the wave is advancing.

The educators responding to the "doing" question at least seem tacitly to endorse the concept of well-being. They are bolstered by educational philosopher Nel Noddings, whose entire book *Happiness in Education* (2003) is dedicated to well-being and flourishing as the only goal of education that makes sense for our world today. In a similar fashion, Richard Ryan and Veronika Huta (2006), in discussing how seeking a life of well-being counteracts the growth of materialistic values, comment that "the topic of *eudaimonia* [well-being] is ever more relevant and timely" (p. 166).

The word *flourishing* goes a step beyond well-being, even though it is occasionally employed as a synonym. For its use here I rely on a definition in line with Scherto Gill and Garrett Thomson (2012), who describe flourishing as "more dynamic [than well-being]. It carries the idea that when a person's life is going well, the various parts work together in a mutually supportive way...like a plant that is flowering" (p. 124). It is as if well-being were the fertile ground that enables roots to take hold and grow, while flourishing is the flowering bud nourished by those roots. Well-being is general; its characteristics apply to a wide sample of individuals; with possible rare exceptions, these characteristics are needed by all of us if we are to become our most fully functioning selves. But the way a flourishing life manifests itself is very particular, it is different for each individual. Flourishing is the best example of what each of us, in our own individual way, is capable of becoming. Flourishing seems to be what the administrators were describing in their wishes that a graduate would "pursue her passions and dreams, contributing to a more equitable world" or "actualizing their gifts and passions for the betterment of all."

What about character education?

How does all this relate to character education, or moral education, or social-emotional learning—or whatever else a school calls its initiative to foster the socially responsible attitudes and actions of tomorrow's citizens? The fact is that what we perceive to be the purpose of our profession influences how we interact with students and peers. Character education needs a discerned, identified purpose if our efforts are to be maximally effective. What schools call their endeavors does not seem to affect the answer. I've spent the past several years asking about purpose in schools and searching the writings of moral and character educators for it, with meager results. The *Journal of Character Education*'s inaugural issue in 2014, for example, invited a number of well known figures working in the field of positive youth development to reflect on the state and future of the field. They did so from a variety of compelling perspectives, but with little apparent consensus on the ultimate goal of the endeavors they were writing about. In their statements that referred to goals or purpose, authors noted such aspirations as halting the moral decline of contemporary society, improving academic achievement, creating a positive school culture or climate, developing strong moral compasses, and fostering the development of citizens for a democratic nation, among other possibilities.

What is the ultimate purpose of these character development initiatives? My answer to that question lies in the final four words of the purpose-of-education statement above, *in the wider community*. Our initiatives for character development should focus on helping kids be sensitive to the well-being of others, so they want to act in ways that foster the well-being of all, and they have the basic skills to do their part to further the process. Some say that a person of character is a person who can be counted on to "do the right thing." What is the right thing, after all, other than looking deeply into a person or situation, asking "what does this person/situation truly need," and then acting on it?

Character development for most educators concerns teaching the skills of how to live with others in ways that foster their well-being. Respect, responsibility, hard work, empathy, democratic citizenship, integrity, curtailing bullying, and all the rest are but (important) pieces of this broader goal. The danger of putting focus on the individual pieces without conscious awareness of the ultimate goal of well-being is like the zen student who kept looking at his master's finger instead of at the moon to which it pointed. As we set goals for character (the topic of the next chapter), it becomes all the more important to keep looking through the lens just described, the lens focusing on what conditions best foster the skills and dispositions to live a life of well-being, and, more importantly from the perspective of morality, what conditions best help students want to support the well-being of others. This is the moon. It's okay to notice the finger, but the moon is the point.

The school that keeps well-being always in focus is not devaluing academics—nor is it devaluing the arts or athletics or social events. Rather, it is sharpening the focus.

Let there be no mistake: in no way does a purpose statement focusing on well-being and individual flourishing diminish the role of academics in school. A challenging academic curriculum is essential in the pursuit of well-being. Challenge is not just a good idea, it is a human need for intellectual as well as all other kinds of growth. Similarly, the skills of literary analysis, historical criticism, and the scientific method are of crucial importance to the intellectual and academic growth of a large portion of the students in our schools. Preparation for college and the world of work are likewise essential for the full development of many.

The school that keeps well-being always in focus is not devaluing academics—nor is it devaluing the arts or athletics or social events.

Rather, it is sharpening the focus; it is asking why and how we focus on academics, why and how we want our students to participate in athletics, and what we want them to get out of dances or clubs, ceramics or painting, community service or student government. A school that expects all its students go to a four-year college, or that wants to train all its students to get high paying jobs, either serves its students well or does its students a disservice. If students pass through the school thinking that a college degree or a high-paying job is the goal, then the school is doing its students, and all of society, a disservice. If, on the other hand, the world of higher education and the world of work are interpreted as possibly important—but not necessarily essential—steps toward leading a meaningful, fulfilling life, then perhaps a service has been done. Of course, we want the majority of our students to develop their minds in the ways that a university education makes possible, and we want all our students to have the financial resources to provide for their needs and the needs of those who depend on them, but such learning and financial resources are too often talked about as if they were the ends in themselves, and thus students get robbed of the truly richer goals. We want students to aim for the moon, but we may inadvertently be giving them the finger.

Finally, there is one advantage for both education in general, and character development in particular, that makes compelling sense in this inner-focused, other-directed purpose of education. The third of the three premises mentioned above (the box on page 10) relates to students. They are the ones we hope will embody our goals, so we will probably have a better chance of getting those goals embodied if our students know what the goals are.

Frequently articulated goal statements like creating a moral compass in kids, arresting the moral decline of society, and even creating life-long learners, are readily accepted by many students. But it is usually not the easily-won-over group that are the primary concern of character educators; the hardest to win over are the angry, the alienated, the disengaged. And frankly, alienated kids are not predisposed to lunge toward goals of community enhancement when those goals are set by the same adults they see as causing their alienation. After all, what's in it for them? On the other hand, when their individual, autonomously-discerned flourishing is seen as the ultimate goal, incentives become stronger, especially for the self-centered. Thereafter, the implications of the need for the individual to support well-being in wider society becomes more reasonable, and perhaps more palatable. Supporting flourishing in students is not support for egocentrism; rather, individuals who flourish become more prosocial (as noted, e.g., by Ryan et al., 2008; McHosky, 1999; Sheldon & McGregor, 2000; Brown & Kasser, 2004). Individuals who fit Ryff's well-being descriptors are those who least lean toward self-centeredness.

Since this is a book specifically about structuring moral, ethical, or character education initiatives for the purpose of promoting well-being, let us now turn more directly to the structural implication of such initiatives. While doing so, however, readers should keep this first lens in mind, because it is the lens of purpose. Whatever the articulated goals are, the primary purpose of *character education* cannot aim at control of behavior at school, because that is not what this field is about. Better classroom behavior is, we hope, one result of good work in character development, but our real aim should be the ongoing growth of self-managed, goal-directed young people who are sensitive to the needs of others and who want to act in such a way that others, as well as themselves, to have the opportunity to flourish.

3

Identifying Goals

Try a short exercise. When you reach the period at the end of this sentence, stop and tell yourself what your school's primary goal for character development is; don't take more than 10 seconds to do this.

Clarity and Articulation of Goals

As stated in the last chapter, we have a better chance of reaching our goals if we know what our goals are. I am amazed at the number of educators I encounter whose schools have programs for character development, but who cannot say what those programs aim to accomplish. Thus the exercise you just experienced. Why the 10-second rule? The time limit is purely arbitrary, but 10 seconds is quite long when you count it out. Think about how long it takes to name the most important sport at your school, or the most important administrator after the principal or head of school. In most cases these categories probably take only three or four seconds of reflection, and then two seconds to articulate the response. Even if most people have to take the time to ask whether the question regards their opinion of which sport is most important or which sport attracts the most spectators, they can answer the question within the 10 seconds. On the other hand, if it takes over 8 seconds to recall what your character goals are, your goals may not be very well identified.

Most coaches of major sports in schools can tell you immediately what their offense is working on right now, and what the defense is working on. But most members of the "team" looking toward character development are less articulate. If we can get clarity on our goals, we may have a better chance of achieving them.

As noted in the previous chapter, the approach outlined here encourages schools to set, clarify, and be aware of goals for moral/ethical/character development by encouraging educators to look through three successive, mutually supportive lenses. Each lens answers a different question.

What are we really aiming for?

The first lens, outlined in the last chapter, is really the most important of the three, because it asks the question *Is the goal moral?* Its endpoint is to help students be attentive to the well-being of those around them. If you did not "buy" the well-being rationale, then use your argument against it to lead you to the purpose statement that most makes sense. If you cannot articulate what the purpose of your endeavors are, you'll be walking down a foggy path. You need to know what you are aiming for.

Is this already a part of our school's DNA?

The second lens asks if the goal aligns with the social or moral components of the school's mission statement. Schools have mission statements both to outline what they most want to focus on, and to distinguish themselves from one another. A mission statement may be analogous to a filter on a camera lens, which cuts out certain kinds of light, or affects in some other way how what is focused on might be interpreted. No mission statement should disagree with the purpose-of-education statement in the last chapter—*to foster in students the skills, and the will, to nurture their own well-being and that of the wider community*—but a school's individual statement of mission/goals may have a particular angle of this statement that, for a number of rich reasons, might breathe interesting life into it.

Do we have community-specific concerns that will be addressed?

The third lens asks if there are challenges facing students, or concerns about school culture, that impact growth or the sense of community at school, or that impede progress toward goals seen through the first two lenses.

This lens should be considered less essential than the others, but if such problems or concerns exist, they are more powerfully addressed in a school where work on them is seen as emerging through the lens of the school's mission statement and the deeper goals the school has set.

The second lens: goals in the school's mission

Though not all schools have a mission statement, nearly every independent school and a growing number of public schools or school districts in North America now have one. A mission statement is a formal declaration of the school's aims, of how the school hopes to, or intends to, shape its students. Most schools post their mission statement on their website. It stands there as a declaration to prospective parents, to the community, to the world, that "this is who we are; this is what we do; this is what your money is paying for; this is what we want to accomplish with the young people entrusted to our care."

Though there are occasional exceptions, an overwhelming majority of mission statements have two parts. One part is academic; it might refer to intellectual advances, to college preparation, or to lifelong learning, but in a nutshell it says "our mission is to instill in students the attitudes and skills of academic excellence."

What we call the "other half" of the mission statement says something about the moral, ethical, or spiritual qualities or skills characteristic of the young people the school wants to graduate. In other words, most school mission statements want not just skilled end users of academic information, they also want good people: they want responsible citizens, people of conscience, leaders of integrity, they want their graduates to be exemplars of social justice, to contribute to the creation of a better world.

Here are a few relatively typical mission statements, as examples. The school names are fictitious, but the elements of their missions are seen widely. The first statement is probably too general, unless the school fills in specific details elsewhere, but it is not uncommon, and it does illustrate the point about mission statements addressing more than just academics. The second and third statements are a little more descriptive; they offer a (slightly) clearer sense of the school's non-academic goals.

Bentster School educates the whole child: body, mind, and spirit.

The Corlen School's mission is to prepare young people to be lifelong learners and responsible citizens for tomorrow's world.

At Vohnsen Academy we challenge students to fulfill both their intellectual potential and their capacity to lead compassionately in their local, national, and world communities.

Some mission statements, as in this next example, include a lot of non-mission verbiage, so you need to know how to wade through the excess:

The Spooner School, located on 162 acres of wooded hillside overlooking the Rockies, is a century-old non-denominational college preparatory school for students in grades 6 through 12 that offers the only accredited global studies program in the West. With classrooms connected to sister schools in nine countries on three different continents and the mandatory study of two foreign languages, our students emerge both ready for college and prepared to meet tomorrow's world as ethically rigorous innovators and respectful team players for a global economy.

Most of the Spooner School's statement describes the school's history, curriculum, and location. After we cut through the descriptions, the real purpose of the school, its mission, shows up in the last half of the second sentence: to prepare students for college, and to prepare students not just to be innovators, but to be "ethically rigorous" innovators; and not just team players, but team players who are exemplary in the ways they look upon and treat others.

Presumably, then, missions outline goals, and many of these goals fit into the social, moral, ethical domains. If the school cares deeply enough about these goals to post them publicly, then the same goals should, in some way, figure into the character goals the school plans intentionally to work on. If they don't, let's hope that the school has thought through this discrepancy and has a reason for it. One reason might arise out of the third lens.

Before we turn to that third lens, though, let's look back at the first two for purposes of alignment. Since the long-term goal, the first lens, is one of lasting, intrinsically motivated behavior sensitive to the well-being of others, two things follow when we look at how the mission statement might inform that ultimate objective. The first is that character goals informed by the mission statement should be goals that align specifically with that first lens. Occasionally, words show up in mission statements that can be interpreted in a moral/ethical way, or not. For example, focusing on "excellence," or preparing students to lead "successful" lives, may have meant one thing to those who penned the mission statement, but something else to someone reading the statement who was not present for its construction. As a case in point, the Josephson Institute of Ethics reported survey results involving 23,000 students—an impressive number—from across the United

States in 2012. One item looked at the perceived connection between cheating and success via this statement posed to students: "In the real world, successful people do what they have to do to win, even if others consider it cheating." Fifty-seven percent of American high school students agreed with the statement, thus indicating their agreement that "if you want to be successful, you have to be willing to do what some people consider cheating." So at school, concepts like success need to be defined in terms of ethical life if they are to be used as character goals. If a "successful life" is in a school's mission statement, that school might strive to make sure its students understand that success is more than a large salary and an expensive automobile.

The second thing that follows concerns whether a mission-related goal is really a character goal. Let's take Corlen School's citizenship as an example. Citizenship can be characterized by a number of quite different activities. Responsible citizens vote; before they vote, responsible citizens inform themselves regarding candidates and issues. Responsible citizens pay their taxes; if they feel their taxes are unfair, they let their opinions be known to the appropriate parties. Most people would also say that responsible citizens look out for their neighbors, that they lend a helping hand when neighbors are in need, and that they respect certain rules of propriety—the conventions of living in society. The list goes on.

Some of these examples of "responsible citizenship" clearly fit through the first lens, the lens of concern for the well-being of others; other examples may or may not fit, depending on how we interpret them. Many elementary schools that address citizenship are much more concerned with helpful and respectful daily behaviors—most of which are moral concerns—than with future political involvement. The important point for our purposes here is that, to be considered character goals, mission-related goals must be seen in a moral/ethical light. If sharing opinions about unfair taxes with elected representatives is not deemed a moral/ethical issue, it still can be an educational goal for the school; it just should not receive attention for character development. The same applies to communication with elected representatives; if the school considers such communication to be a moral/ethical issue, it then has a responsibility to address it from the perspective of social responsibility, justice, equity, or something of the sort, so that students see the connection. More importantly, if citizenship is a character goal at the school, it should focus on those aspects of participating in community most associated with fostering the well-being of others.

The third lens: worries, needs, and emergencies

A third lens concerns more immediate issues or behaviors that arise at school, especially regarding how students interact with others; this includes respectful behavior, responsible compliance with the needs of community life, and possibly even issues like graffiti and treatment of property. This lens requires first that we distinguish items of ethical concern from other kinds of concern. Depression, for example, is a concern, as are the numbers of students who come to school hungry, or the amount of sleep some students get; but these are not necessarily moral education concerns.

Unfortunately, other pressing needs do arise, and when they do they must be reckoned with. It is not uncommon for good schools to realize that they have "a plagiarism problem," or "a social media problem," or some other behavioral or school culture issue insidious enough to distract from the work of the school. These problems sometimes need to be addressed before mission-focused character work can continue. For example, either the Corlen School or Vohnsen Academy might one day become aware of a chronic problem regarding use of drugs, or widespread cheating. For good reason, these schools might decide that a formal program to address the issue of academic integrity—or to impart information about drugs and their effects, and to teach emotional management, or the skills involved in resisting peer pressure—might be a more important use of energies, until improvement is seen, than sustained work on responsible citizenship (at Corlen) or compassionate leadership (at Vohnsen Academy).

Identifying such "emergency needs" as character goals can be completely appropriate, as long as sight is not lost of the fact that the school still has a mission and goals seen through that first lens, and thus that any interventions should be planned to complement, or at least not to impede, work toward the essential, long-term goal of concern for the well-being of others. Moreover, a certain amount of evidence suggests that work toward well-being by addressing the issues that make up the Guts part of this book can help inoculate students against pressures to engage in maladaptive behaviors (see e.g., Roth et al., 2010, regarding bullying; Bureau & Mageau, 2014, regarding honesty in general; and Jordan, 2001, for cheating).

The same is true of other needs, beyond emergencies. The framework for selecting goals offered here is a suggestion. There may be a variety of reasons why other, non-mission related goals are chosen; the choice is up to each individual school. But do something that you can articulate! Have goals that people know about, that they buy into, and that they want to contribute to developing. Moreover, make sure that work toward the goals leads to the internalization of the values they represent. Draconian measures can diminish the prevalence of bullying, or cheating, or substance use, but if moral growth is the purposeful work of the school, adopt procedures not on the basis of what might achieve short-term results, but rather on the basis of what maximizes the chances of long-term positive development.

Daily irritations versus character concerns

Some educators try to push daily irritations to the forefront of character concerns when their schools are setting goals. Such irritations can be seductive because teachers, especially teachers with large class loads, are overwhelmed by certain student behaviors, or lack thereof. The dress code fits this category at many schools, as do issues like students not coming to class on time, not coming to class prepared, or not following any of a number of rules theoretically constructed to help life proceed smoothly, like keeping to the right in the hallway or bussing dirty trays and dishes in the cafeteria.

Many behaviors that irritate teachers fall under the subheading of "respect and responsibility," but not every action related to respect or responsibility is necessarily a moral issue, in the sense of an issue related to justice, rights, or the well-being of others (Nucci, 2001, 2009). For example, I recently visited a high school where a faculty survey identified the most pressing character concern as students' responsibility for coming to assemblies and other meetings on time. Is this a moral issue, a mission-related character or ethical issue, or a daily irritation that fits through the two large and more important lenses only with difficulty?

Lenses can be helpful in deciding whether such irritations deserve, or not, to be treated as character goals. It's important to look at minor disturbing behaviors with as much objectivity as can be mustered, because in some cases they are indeed character development issues, and in others they are annoyances rather than moral or ethical concerns.

One way to winnow a large number of possible goals is to lay them out and see which most easily fit through the three lenses described. Some annoyances go through all three smoothly (e.g., treatment of younger students or cutting into the lunch line) while others might need more effort (completion of homework or talking without raising one's hand). How, and whether, student responsibility for arriving on time at assemblies fits the framework above needs ultimately to be made at the school level. Since the mission statement of the school I visited spoke to global citizenship, faculty working for character development might most easily see the common purpose of their work by addressing student responsibility through the lens of our socio-moral responsibilities toward those with whom we live, as citizens in a community. Our fellow community members need to know if they can count on us to be somewhere; our relationships are influenced by how we fulfill such mutual expectations. Well-being is best fostered in relationships of trust and support.

Note that refocusing, as just described, is not just a matter of tweaking language. The school irritated by students not coming to assemblies or meetings on time has a variety of options at its disposal, some of which could bring about behavioral control (timely arrival at meetings) but do such in a way that increases anger, frustration, or a sense of injustice on the part of students. Some of these measures that produce detrimental results happen also to be enticing because they show quick results, or are easy to administer. They are the proverbial easy way out. But the short-term results may undermine, or even impede, long-term growth in the moral/ethical domain.

Putting the lenses together

So how do we get from point A to point C, meaning from the point where we realize we need a formal initiative for character development (or to be more intentional in our current initiative) to the point where we have our goals fully defined and implemented? It starts with deciding which, from among all possible goals, we want first to set as ours. Here is one possible process, out of a number of others. Regardless of the process used, though, it almost always works best if it takes place within a good committee.

1. Identify what ethical, moral, character education concerns exist in the community

Are there pressing issues of general concern? Don't try too hard to find them; if they don't show up quickly and easily, they are not pressing. But do listen to all that are expressed. In a recent workshop where participants were asked to identify their personal views of "the most important character issues to focus on with students," the following list was generated. We'll use it as an example:

getting over selfishness
cheating
social jockeying
increasing autonomy
always comparing themselves with others
empathy & compassion
students' sense of entitlement
developing empathy
bullying
making the school a welcoming place

2. Decide if the issue is a moral issue

Run the list of concerns through the lens of well-being, "is this a moral issue or not?" See if committee members are able to identify, and to let go of, some of the items that—regardless of how prevalent or irritating they might be—should not be considered character development goals at the present time. Are the issues on the list moral/ethical concerns, or do they fit into the category of irksome and worrisome, but not of a moral nature? One way to distinguish, which many find helpful, comes from moral development expert Larry Nucci's work with children (Nucci, 2001, 2009). Ask "if there were no rules about this, would it be all right to do it?" Moral issues are right or wrong regardless of whether there is a rule. For example, if a school had no rules about pushing younger children off the swings or about taking someone else's lunch money, would it be all right to do so? Respondents over the age of five overwhelmingly assert that it is not all right; even if a teacher said it was okay, they maintain, both pushing and stealing are wrong. Thus, they are moral issues.

On the other hand, if a school had no rules about teachers' names, would it be wrong, or would it be all right, for second graders to call their teacher, Mrs. Emory, by her first name, Susan? Would it be wrong, or all right, Nucci asks, for Mrs. Emory's students to chew gum in class?

Most respondents would say that either of these behaviors is fine as long as the school has no rule to the contrary. In other words, what makes these examples (called "conventional" issues rather than moral issues) right or wrong is the presence or absence of a rule, in contrast to the moral issues in the preceding paragraph, which are right or wrong in and of themselves, regardless of whether there is a rule. Conventional issues can be used as character concerns, but generally moral issues should take precedence, because they are less subject to change over time, because there is more societal consensus on their importance, and more importantly, because students will buy into them more readily.

Most readers would look at the workshop list of character concerns on the previous page and see nearly all issues as moral issues; the possible exceptions might be "increasing autonomy," "comparing themselves with others," and "sense of entitlement," depending on what is meant by entitlement, and whether the sense of entitlement is acted on. A sense of autonomy, though not a moral issue per se, turns out to be a critical issue in moral development, and will be revisited in the Guts part of this book; let's set it aside for now. Similarly, let's set aside students comparing themselves to others, as long as it does not manifest itself in negative personal interactions.

If a definition of entitlement is discussed, we might discover that for certain members of the committee the word refers to an attitude that "I'm better than other people so I do not need to follow the same rules." In this context entitlement does fit Nucci's moral/ethical category, as an issue of fairness; rules that promote well-being in the community should be followed. So we'll leave entitlement on the list of goals, but I would prefer to rephrase it, since the "I'm better and thus more privileged than others" is set up in such a way that we see how negative results will ensue. Rather, we should look toward a positive outcome by aiming for our ultimate goal, something akin to all of us working together, interacting positively, and on relatively equal footing. A term like "collaborative interdependence," or "collaborative support," might work; the committee may prefer different wording, but I'll use the phrase collaborative interdependence for now.

3. Choose the most appropriate fit with the mission statement

After the list is filtered through the first lens, the moral lens, look at the remaining items through the lens of the school's mission statement. If you don't have a mission statement, this step can be skipped, and some mission statements are not explicit enough to be helpful in this regard, like Bentster School's "body, mind, and spirit" above. Let's say we're going through this exercise at Vohnsen Academy, where "capacity to lead compassionately" is one of our mission-stated aims. Of the items remaining on the list above—selfishness, cheating, social jockeying, empathy and compassion, bullying, collaborative interdependence, and making the school a welcoming place— some probably have a more direct bearing on the mission to lead compassionately than others.

Given Vohnsen Academy's mission for "compassionate leadership," both empathy and compassion, from this list, have direct bearings, so we should keep them as a combined goal of empathy/compassion. Cheating is less directly tied to the mission, so let's set it aside for now. The next step would be to look at the remaining items for "most appropriate fit": social jockeying, bullying, collaborative interdependence, and making the school a welcoming place. If choosing Vohnsen Academy's goals were up to me, I would opt for "making the school a welcoming place" as one of them. I see bullying and a welcoming school as two sides of the same coin, so I'm fine dropping bullying. We'll be working toward the same kind of school culture: there is no bullying in a school that is truly welcoming. I would also tend to keep collaborative interdependence, because of the interpersonal work needed for the good "leadership" called for in VA's mission.

Note that the three goals now identified—empathy/compassion, welcoming environment, and collaborative interdependence—all fit with our mission statement's goal of compassionate leadership. Moreover, we have already fit the character development goals through our key lens, that set of characteristics that best allow the human spirit to flourish, that best allows each of us feel like he or she is developing in an individual, positive, and noble way. It is clear that neither good leadership nor well-being develops effectively unless we are in supportive, compassionate, welcoming environments. The three goals fit nicely.

4. Select a number of goals that is feasible

Is there an ideal number of goals for character development? I've never seen research on the subject, but common wisdom seems to suggest two or three specific goals, up to a maximum of perhaps five. Ideally, a school should look at three guides regarding numbers: 1) pick only as many as people can remember, 2) pick only as many as you can realistically work toward, and 3) pick only as many as you can track. Then pick the lowest of those three numbers. If your talented community could easily remember nine goals, but could only track six of them, and you only have time and energy to work toward three of the six, then pick three.

Before addressing a few miscellaneous issues that close this chapter, let's imagine my being faced, as a fictitious member of Vohnsen Academy's character development committee, with the question that opened this chapter. The question was: What is your school's top goal for character development? I've got three goals to choose from, culled from a larger list of community concerns: fostering a sense of compassion, creating an authentically welcoming environment, and collaborative interdependence. It takes me three seconds to name them. I've got three seconds to decide which is most important in my opinion, and I will need only two seconds to give my answer. Total time elapsed: 8 seconds. It's not so hard after the preliminary work of deciding on goals is done.

Miscellaneous issues

The advantage of a team

To be fair, let's remember that the goals just described are the preferences of a committee consisting of a single person, the writer of these words. Real decisions about goals are best made by groups. In the chapter on "permeation" we'll discuss that second premise, that we have better chances of reaching our goals when we work on them as a team. My team—the committee—may opt for different goals than I. Whatever goals we choose, we will probably have a better chance of meeting them, and they probably will be of better quality, if they are chosen by a group rather than by an individual. Common wisdom and practice also tell us that goals chosen by a community have a better chance of buy-in from the comumunity.

Non-mission related goals

It may happen that the committee feels a need for choosing some goal that is not covered by a mission statement, as discussed above. This is feasible, as long as the goal is compatible with the mission statement. For example, I set cheating aside in my discussion above. It may be that the committee feels that issues of academic integrity need to be addressed. The fairness and trust component of integrity certainly is a moral issue, so the committee should have its wish. That being said, the more clearly goals can be seen through all three lenses, the greater the energy the community will muster to accomplish them.

Rarely, but occasionally, a school says "We don't have any salient problems, but we think character development is important for student growth. What should we use as goals?" Always keep those first two lenses in mind: the lens of well-being comes first; you may, or may not, want to shape moral goals on your school's mission. My personal counsel to the school with no pressing issues would be to focus on fostering students' perception of the autonomy they have, on expanding circles and depth of relationships, and on specific social, emotional, academic and purpose-focusing competencies, per the second part of this book. My reasoning is this: there are character development benefits galore to be gleaned from such work, in addition to academic motivation benefits and growth toward well-being.

Head, Heart, and Hand

Character educators often refer to the head, heart, and hand of character, which educator Tom Lickona, following Aristotle, refers to as knowing the good, desiring the good, and doing the good. We should want students (and ourselves) to know what the goals are (what well-being is, its application to one's life and the lives of others), to feel like accomplishing or "living" the goals, and to have the skills necessary to live the goals.

Let's take a school with concerns about bullying, by way of example. The immediate goal is to stop unkind behavior, of course, but success in reaching the goal will come more easily if the head, the heart, and the hand are all considered. That is, the school will have more success curtailing bullying 1) if kids understand what constitutes bullying and how it affects both individuals and the community in general; 2) if kids have the skills to resist going along with the crowd, the skills to extricate themselves from uncomfortable social situations, the skills to resolve conflicts, and a few other skills; and 3) if the climate of the school is one where students generally like their peers (and themselves, too) and are disposed—because they like themselves and the people they are at school with—to work to create and maintain positive relationships. Most school character initiatives are efficient in dealing with the "head" part; teaching the intellectual content kids need to know: that bullying behavior is harmful, that it makes kids feel bad, that it's important to tell an adult if you're being bullied, that bystanders can and should remove their support for the bully... and all the other things kids should know. But very few students have problems with the head aspect of character growth. It's the other two parts that are more problematic. The "hand" includes all the skills young people should master to interact positively. Kids who tend to be targets for bullies can often diminish their "desirability" as targets by learning certain skills. Sometimes these include personal hygiene skills, and more frequently they include social interaction skills like how to start conversations, how to make friends, how to compliment others, how to defuse tense situations.

Kids who are bullies may suffer from some of the same skill deficits as those who are bullied, but they may have other issues, too, like inadequate problem solving skills or the inability to take another person's perspective. What skills need to be taught depends on the individual in question; that's one reason why there is an art to doing this kind of work, and to being an educator in general. There is much more evidence that behaviors can be improved, long term, through teaching skills than there is through transferring knowledge or information, though the two complement one another.

The third part of the character triad is what we call the "heart." Sometimes kids misbehave because they did not know something was wrong, or did not understand; in character work, these are "head" issues. But in most cases kids (and adults) understand (the head), and they even have the skills to do the right thing (the hand), they just do not feel like doing it. They act out of hurt, frustration, selfishness, or feeling like they were treated unfairly. The disposition to act with the benefit of others in mind is what we call the heart. Any program for character development that wants to be successful instilling long term helpful behaviors must work on the heart part of the equation; this will be the subject of the second part of this book, what we call the Guts. Though the heart is neglected in school programs even more than the head and the hand, there is considerable documentation on how to catalyze the internalization of positive behaviors and attitudes.

4

Packaged Programs

As chapter two began with an exercise (naming your most important character goal), let's start this one with a different exercise. Pick a number between one and a hundred.

Our office occasionally gets a phone call from a school reporting a recent decision, or a renewed commitment, to work on character; they are calling to ask if we can recommend a good program. Programs for character education come in two basic varieties. "Home grown" refers to initiatives organized in-house, with a school's own talents and resources; "packaged programs" are those developed by others and marketed with instructions, materials, and frequently training, where an expert comes to the school to make sure the program is understood and can be implemented correctly; many, though not all, have been developed by individuals with considerable expertise. Our office caller is usually asking, then, "Is there a good packaged program you could recommend?" As might be inferred from the previous chapter, the answer is more complicated than the question. The best program depends on a lot of factors.

If the school wants a packaged program, the question should not be "Is there a good packaged program that you would recommend," but rather "Is there a good packaged program for a school like ours?" There are a number of excellent programs for elementary schools, but they are not necessarily appropriate for students at higher developmental levels. And vice-versa. So "a school like ours" means age of students, in addition to the other factors.

In search of "What Works in Character Education," Marvin W. Berkowitz and Melinda Bier (2005) looked at research data for over outcome goals sought by programs / programs showing evidence of effectiveness (Berkowitz & Bier, 2005)

■ strong research evidence
■ moderate research evidence
■ no research evidence of success in this area

a hundred packaged programs for positive youth development. They could find appropriately rigorous studies to document effectiveness in only 33 programs out of that much larger number. Lack of evidence for effectiveness does not necessarily mean a program is bad, but it does raise an important issue. If you're going to devote time and money to a program for character development, and you have a choice between a program with demonstrated results and a program without demonstrated results, which do you pick? You need a pretty good reason if you pick one devoid of research when there is another program that has shown itself to be effective.

Sometimes a member of the character development committee knows someone at another school, where "they're using such-and-such for character and they seem to like it." There's nothing like a satisfied customer, and the fact that teachers at another school like the program does indeed carry weight. As good as it is to know that colleagues elsewhere like a program, though, that still is not sufficient justification for picking a program without demonstrated effectiveness unless there are other, countervailing reasons for its choice.

So one issue to consider is that of age appropriateness, and another is evidence of effectiveness. How teacher-friendly the program is could be a third. But none of these points to the all-important issue that was the subject of the previous chapter. What is it that you want to accomplish? What are your goals? The programs on the market, the programs that Berkowitz and Bier looked at, were not all created with the same goals in mind.

To illustrate this point in workshops, I sometimes ask a random participant to pick a number between 1 and 100, which is the reason for the exercise that opened this chapter. If the poor soul picks her lucky number and it happens to be 61, or 92, or even 34, then my response has to be "pick again, but this time pick a number between 1 and 33"; those programs after number 33 are the ones that had no appropriate evidence that they produce the results they advertise. Such is life; at least such was life in 2005 when Berkowitz and Bier looked at studies. The situation might be better today, but we don't know until we do our homework.

After the participant picks a number between 1 and 33, I then show the group the chart on the page to the left. The numbers across the top of the chart refer to each of the 33 programs Berkowitz and Bier found with demonstrated effectiveness. The dots on the chart mark the

programs showing evidence of effectiveness (Berkowitz & Bier, 2005)

outcome goals sought by programs

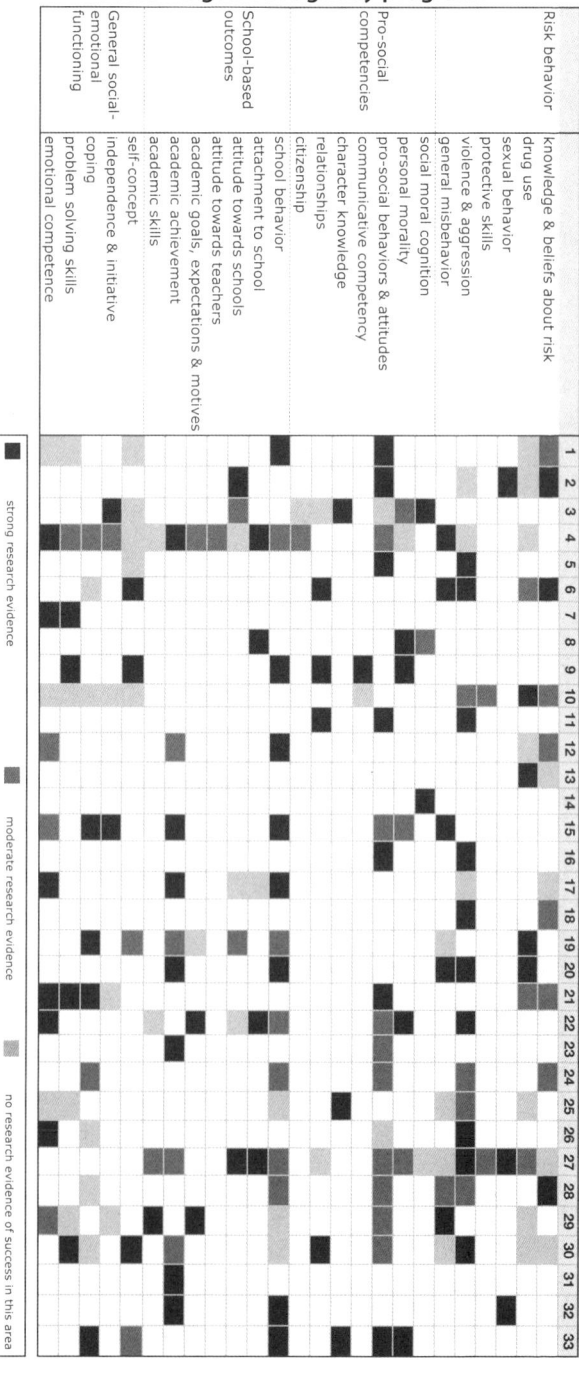

Risk behavior	knowledge & beliefs about risk
	drug use
	sexual behavior
	protective skills
	violence & aggression
	general misbehavior
	social moral cognition
Pro-social competencies	personal morality
	pro-social behaviors & attitudes
	communicative competency
	character knowledge
	relationships
	citizenship
School-based outcomes	school behavior
	attachment to school
	attitude towards schools
	attitude towards teachers
	academic goals, expectations & motives
	academic achievement
	academic skills
General social-emotional functioning	self-concept
	independence & initiative
	coping
	problem solving skills
	emotional competence

■ strong research evidence   ■ moderate research evidence   □ no research evidence of success in this area goals the program was designed to achieve; the very light gray boxes mean that Berkowitz and Bier could find no evidence in the research literature that the program successfully addressed this issue, though it was a program goal. The darker gray boxes indicate that moderate research support was found for that particular aspect of character development, and the black boxes indicate strong support for the area under assessment.

So, let's say the participant picks the number 20, the number for a program that does show evidence of effectiveness. Number 20 has five black boxes, representing areas with strong support of effectiveness. Only a few other programs out of the 33 show such strength. So is program number 20 a good program for the participant's school? Well, that depends. As the discussions from the previous chapter and this one suggest, the answer to the question regarding the appropriateness of number 20 depends on how its boxes—areas of effectiveness— match up with what the school wants to accomplish, the goals.

The chart we just looked at is reproduced to the left here, but this time the left hand column is filled in with the competency area represented by each letter. The areas where program 20 shows evidence of strength include the program's effects on diminishing 1) drug use, 2) violence and aggression, and 3) general misbehavior like theft & vandalism, defiance of adult authority, and gang activity. Program 20 also has shown to lead to 4) fewer acting out behaviors (skipping school, breaking rules, and general classroom comportment); and 5) improved academic achievement (Berkowitz & Bier, 2005).

If those are the behaviors your school is targeting, then program 20 might indeed be a great match (assuming you are an elementary school, since that is the age group program 20 was created for). A school more interested in what we call areas of prosocial competency, though, as many of our schools are, might steer in another direction, since program 20 showed no evidence in prosocial competency (rows G - M). Prosocial competency includes skills and traits like moral reasoning, taking responsibility for one's interpersonal actions, empathy, caring and concern for others, and so forth. If behaviors like these are a school's goals, then programs like 3 (for middle school), or 9 and 33 (for elementary grades) seem to be better matches than 20.

The names of all 33 programs addressed in Berkowitz and Bier's research report (2005) may be found on pages 13-16 of the PDF document at http://www.rucharacter.org/file/practitioners_518.pdf.

The point here, where we are looking at process, is the critical role played by deciding on goals before choosing a plan of action. Whether you want to purchase a program and go with the training it suggests, or whether you want to use the many talents and skills of your school's staff and perhaps the wider community, you need to be intentional in the way you proceed. You have to have a plan. You have to have goals. It's not just a question of which programs are good; it's a question of which programs are good for which goals, in which school.

5

Permeation

Let's go back to the exercise at the beginning of chapter 2, which asked you to articulate your primary character goal in 10 seconds. Imagine five respected, but randomly selected, colleagues from your school. Could they do the exercise in the same time frame? And if they could, would they identify the same goal?

At issue here is the second premise:

We have a better chance of reaching our goals if we work together as a team.

If a culture of character is what a school wants, that culture will not emerge via spontaneous generation. It will take shape to the extent that work toward it permeates all facets of school life. The number of individuals who know and understand the goals, and who are willing to support the cause, matters, as does the extent to which their efforts are aligned. So permeation in our context refers to numbers, alignment, and perseverance.

Permeation in numbers

If the individual designated as "character education coordinator" is the only person working to reach a school's character development goals (as is sadly the case in some schools), an ethical culture probably won't develop at all. With a committee of five people, the chances are better, but still slim. Think about the difference 80% of the adults at school might make, all working toward the same goals, and especially if these 80% are joined by students (see premise three), and by parents. That's permeation.

I once had a tour by a member of the senior class at Kent Denver School in Colorado. I had done my homework, but not wanting to put my guide on the spot, I asked him, somewhat indirectly, if he was aware that the school had character goals. His response came back with such certainty that I thought it okay to press for details. Not only did he fire off Kent Denver's goals, he also assured me that just about anyone in the senior class would offer me exactly the same goals. He was right, as interviews with other students later confirmed.

When I asked the young man how this was possible, he seemed surprised. Permeation was not the word he used, but it was what he described: "What do you mean, how do we know our goals? Every time our headmaster talks to us, he's talking about those goals. We talk about them in class all the time. Even the coaches talk about our goals!" For my guide, there was nothing special about it. My visitor questions bordered on the inane, almost as if I had asked whether students went to class at his school. Dealing with the goals was just the way they did school at Kent Denver.

Permeation in programs

Here is another version of the 10-second exercise. Stop for a moment to answer the question "Why does your school have a community service program?"

Five or six replies are most commonly offered to that question, ranging from "We want kids to learn how to give back" and "We want our students to develop a culture of service," all the way to the outlier "It helps get them into good colleges." The problem is that when I have asked this question—to educators in probably fifty schools—nearly everyone needs time to reflect before offering an answer. As happens when the question regarding the purpose of education is posed, the pause suggests they had never before considered the question, or that they heard the answer so long ago, they could not remember what it was. The responses ultimately offered are all nice, but they seem to be "educated guesses." Try it sometime; ask a few randomly selected colleagues. Are they guessing at the answer, or do they know it? Do their answers match yours? Do they match one another? The question about community service here points beyond sheer numbers, to a second dimension of permeating a culture: alignment of programs.

Structure & Guts of Character Education

The rocket ship below is a visual metaphor we sometimes use in workshops. The student is there, ready to blast off into a future of promise, his own propulsion system ready to fire up. Compare that illustration with the one on the next page, where the student is surrounded and supported by a wide variety of metaphorical guidance and propulsion systems: parents, advisory or homeroom, arts and athletic programs, academic rigor. When all these are aligned with a common purpose in view, when each knows its function in the larger scheme of things, that's another dimension of permeation: permeation via program alignment.

The problem is that most schools are not as "together" as this, as the varied responses to the "why community service" question only start to illustrate. Though permeation via numbers is a key factor in the extent to which a culture of character will take shape, good work takes more than just active bodies. Saturating a culture with new ideas and practices happens—results sink deeper—when both a critical mass of individuals engage and when their efforts support and complement one another. By way of further illustration, compare the "good rocket"

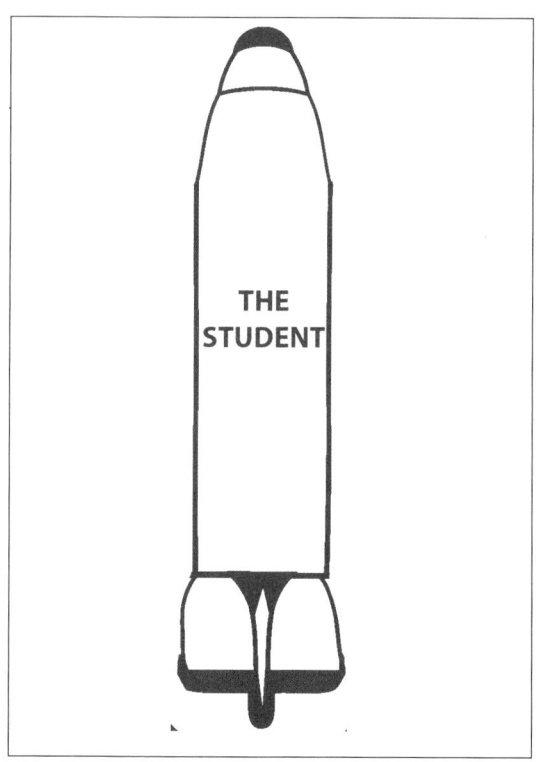

below—the ship most schools wish they were—with "bad rocket" on page 48. Bad rocket is, sadly, a metaphor for many schools, as evidenced by the number of educators who look at it with a smile of embarrassed recognition. Bad rocket schools (some schools are not quite that bad) have all the programs: well organized community service, an honor system, an active parent group, rigorous academics, and more; moreover, these programs are often headed by competent, caring, energetic professionals. It's just that, too often, the people involved are so busy working with their programs that they don't remember either the program's primary purpose or its ideal contribution to the school's broader goals. The result is what we refer to as "silos of genius, (but) communal underperformance."

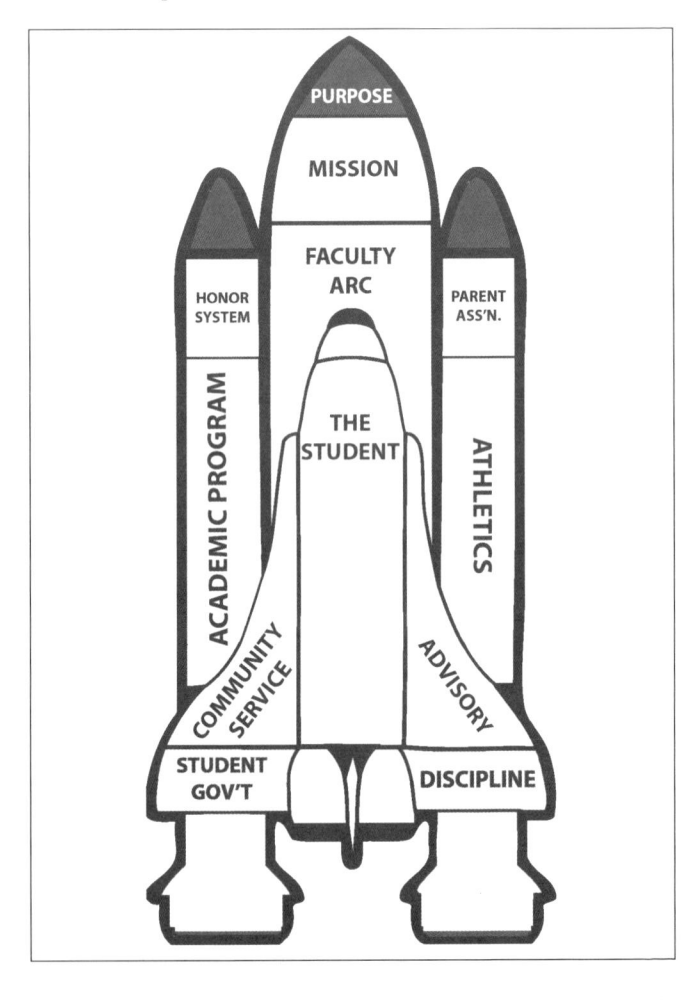

If a school has an agreed-upon purpose, the task to be accomplished, then, is gradually, intentionally, to move as many of those essential program pieces as possible into alignment with that purpose. Let's go back to the mission of The Corlen School from the past chapter, as an example:

The Corlen School's mission is to prepare young people to be lifelong learners and responsible citizens for tomorrow's world.

Ideally, then, nearly everything done at Corlen is intentionally focused on academic growth and one or the other of the school's two stated goals (if not all on three): lifelong learning, and the kind of responsible citizenship that nurtures the well-being of the community as a whole.

What about community service? If I were an administrator at Corlen I would like community service—in addition to supporting our academic program to the extent feasible—to aim squarely at reaching one, or both, of the concepts housed in the words *responsible*, and *citizenship*. When members of the Corlen faculty get asked why we have a community service program, answers would be neither pat nor memorized, but they would be immediate, and all would say something like:

Well, our school is all about preparing kids to be responsible citizens for tomorrow's world. We can do lots to further the cause of responsible citizenship through our academic program, but service in the community offers a range of opportunities far beyond what we can do in the English classroom or the science lab. Fostering responsibility for the well-being of the community is a point of eemphasis in the way we organize and execute our service program.

Notice that simply knowing and articulating an answer like this does little to reach the goals at Corlen. Contrary to the conceptual practice at many schools, however, at least the Corlen faculty has a sense of how its program could, and should, be organized, and how it aligns with other activities at the school. Understanding organization also lays the foundations for the coming chapter, on assessment. Because the Corlen faculty understands why the service program exists, teachers know at least some of the assessment questions to ask as they begin to evaluate whether they are achieving their goals.

Those other answers to the "why community service" question might come in later, about kids developing a culture of service, or even about college applications. They are all good; they are all feasible. But

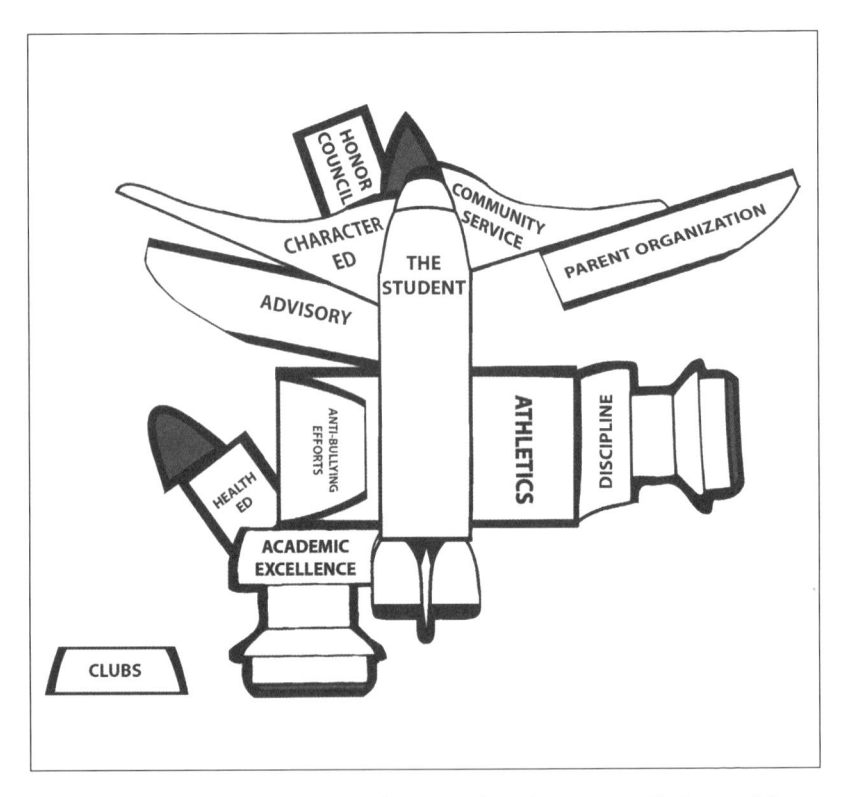

[Figure: A rocket labeled "THE STUDENT" surrounded by components labeled HONOR COUNCIL, CHARACTER ED, COMMUNITY SERVICE, PARENT ORGANIZATION, ADVISORY, ANTI-BULLYING EFFORTS, HEALTH ED, ACADEMIC EXCELLENCE, ATHLETICS, DISCIPLINE, CLUBS.]

this is a school that for reasons of its own has chosen to tell the world that the purpose of its existence is to create responsible citizens, so why toss a golden opportunity out the window by not tapping into the power of organized service to help fulfill that purpose? An interesting service experience, well performed, certainly will look good on a student's college application, and yes, we want our kids to foster positive attitudes toward service in the community, but the primary reason we want them to experience service and develop positive attitudes about being of service to others is that we consider service to be one of the essential avenues of preparation for responsible citizenship. To be more precise about the primary reason, we can look at Corlen's mission statement through the "first lens" discussed in chapter two. We want students to develop positive attitudes about service because service directed toward filling the well-being needs fosters the kind of community that best makes it possible for all—everyone in the community—to flourish.

Adults at Vohnsen Academy, with its mission to nurture compassionate leadership, should articulate their rationale for service in different language than those at Corlen, but with quite similar structure, using a statement something like:

VA is about leadership development, and especially about leadership that is compassionately exercised. We can study leadership academically and we can give kids as many leadership roles as possible, but our community service program is one of the best ways we have to give students a chance to practice leadership in the community, and thus to have first-hand experience with it; and at every turn, we are also doing everything we can to help them lead compassionately.

Note how the mission statement at Vohnsen Academy puts certain obligations on the school that are not necessarily imposed by the statement at The Corlen School. Corlen's service program could, and probably should, give students leadership opportunities. On the other hand, VA is pretty much obligated by its mission to organize community service in such a way that students are involved in leadership development in as many aspects of community service as possible. That's what permeation is all about. Otherwise, the program is not as aligned with the school's mission as it (easily) could be. What Susan Nordenger has done with her community service program at La Jolla Country Day School (California), for example, would be a good model for Vohnsen Academy; it was set up with leadership development specifically in mind. Instead of Nordenger doing all the organizational work for service projects, as happens in many schools, at La Jolla Country Day a committee of 40 sophomores, juniors, and seniors vets, and ultimately approves, every service project the school is going to participate in. If a member of the sophomore class or even the chair of the Board of Trustees became aware of a particularly needy project that would benefit from student attention, they would both follow the same procedure, by presenting an outline of the project to the student committee entrusted with making the decision regarding the project's fit, vis-à-vis the program's goals.

After a service project is completed at La Jolla Country Day, members of that same student committee further the cause of leadership development by evaluating the project formally: how appropriate it was, how well executed it was, what recommendations could be made for the future, and so forth. The evaluation is organized and carried out by students: one leading, the other learning. A junior or senior who has been through the process before, and thus has some expertise, evaluates each project with a sophomore who is now engaged in learning the evaluation process so that he or she can take the lead the following year, with a younger student.

When community service is organized to support the school's character development goals, the level of permeation sinks one degree deeper: it becomes culture; culture fosters character. The rocket ship's various parts align a slight bit more, and the vessel is better equipped to support student journeys to the proposed destination. Goals maximally permeate a school when the sports program, student government, drama and any of a number of other initiatives are aligned such that, to the extent feasible, their activities all aim at accomplishing the school's goals. In elementary schools, this alignment applies also to recess, the lunch room, and time in the hallways, in addition to formal programs.

When Michelle Scandurro became Head of the Upper School at St. Martin's Episcopal School just outside of New Orleans, she and her staff built a vision of their school that saw students taking responsibility for both their education and the community in which their education was unfolding. Among their goals were those of increasing student sensitivity to others in the community, and self-motivated engagement in school. One strategy for reaching those goals entailed fostering student autonomy. Over a period of five years Scandurro, Assistant Head of Upper School Mary Bond, and their colleagues increasingly helped permeate the Saint Martin's culture through the supportive empowerment of students. The process was gradual, but it was incremental and intentional. At St. Martin's, permeation via numbers thus began with the faculty, all working together, envisioning the kind of school they wanted, sharing their vision with students, and giving students an increasing number of roles to play. Permeation via alignment of programs began with the disciplinary system. Here's how.

Before the new administration stepped in at St. Martin's, major disciplinary infractions were adjudicated by a council of three faculty members, plus one additional faculty moderator, and rotating teams of three students. Because the adults were the ones most familiar with the process—and of course because they were adults—the triads of students deferred to the teachers, so whatever recommendations came out of the committee were basically adult recommendations made to adult administrators. As a result of the newer vision, where students would increasingly be engaged in creating the future of their school, the number of adults on the committee was reduced from three to one, and the number of students increased from three to nine. The students were elected for one-year terms, and the added longevity offered them greater experience, more expertise, and of course greater confidence. The one adult became a non-voting moderator for the group.

The way minor disciplinary infractions were handled also changed. This system, too, was purpose focused; with the goal of strengthening relationships in mind, punitive sanctions were either diminished or abolished in cases where punishment was foreseen to improve neither the school climate nor student behavior. Records were kept, and action (frequently non-punitive) did follow when concerns were elevated, but not every transgression of a minor school rule required "consequences." There was no increase in misbehavior when the school took this step, but there was an increase in positive feelings about their school—among both adults and students.

Similar changes, but for the same focused reasons, took place in revamping the high school's advisory program the following year. The third year was devoted to seeking better ways to give students leadership roles, and both to prepare them for these roles and to mentor them along the way. These changes were gradual changes, all part of a five year plan for aligning St. Martin's metaphorical rocket ship in creation of a vehicle to meet the school's vision. The faculty at St. Martins was fostering autonomy in students in ways that both strengthened interpersonal relationships and increased school engagement. Permeation happened.

Getting buy-in from colleagues

Most schools have a small set of individuals who are gung ho and ready to help with character development work. These are the people who know character development is an important aspect of their profession, and in many cases they have the skills, creativity, and energy to make it happen—at least in those areas of the school that are touched by their presence. This enthusiasm and expertise are key to getting things started.

At the other end of the spectrum, most schools also have a faculty member or two, and sometimes a larger number, that are uninterested, or even reluctant to engage in anything that might deviate from the status quo, regardless of how important it might be. Not everyone likes change. Educators are busy; their jobs are stressful; they don't have time for extras. How to enlist the talents of these educators needs to be addressed at the individual level in individually specific ways, because solutions to such problems depend so much on the personalities and situations involved. Sometimes the right words from the Principal or Head of School go a long way. Some schools might prefer to leave the reluctant few aside for now, and focus efforts on a coalition of the willing.

The group in-between is more critical, referring to those who are neither the gung ho early adopters nor the reluctant or disengaged. In most schools this group in the middle is sizable and could go either way; these educators are busy professionals who nevertheless under the right conditions could, and would, be helpful, maybe even excited. At St. Martin's, the problem was minimized (though not completely overcome) because "the boss" was leading the charge. At Lot Whitcomb School permeating took place via another process.

Sometimes the right kind of activity can create energy rather than sap it.

When Marie-Claire Wonacott and Amy Clinton were starting their character work at Lot Whitcomb School (Oregon), they invited colleagues to read a common book and discuss one chapter every two weeks. The first year they wanted to work with Marilyn Watson and Laura Ecken's *Learning to Trust* (2003), because it was a case study of a teacher who worked on developmental discipline "with kids like ours." Wonacott and Clinton wondered, for their colleagues, if maybe they could get ideas on how to work with some of their kids better. About three quarters of the teachers were willing to give the group a try (it split into two groups); they spent two afternoons each month sharing thoughts about the chapter, reflections, and ideas. After hearing how energized discussions were, other teachers joined later. Momentum grew. Permeation happens. Teachers not initially enthusiastic were brought along by the enthusiasm of the original core. It was a group eager to further the goal of "making our school a better place for learning and growing by fostering autonomy, a sense of belonging, and social-emotional-academic competence in kids."

Notice what often happens in scenarios like this. All teachers describe themselves as busy. Nearly all teachers are, in fact, somewhere on that continuum between busy and overwhelmed. Rarely does a teacher have extra time to take on something else. Why would a teacher want to spend their prep time, after students have left the building, discussing a book when neither the book nor giving up their prep time was mandatory? Sometimes the right kind of activity can create energy rather than sap it. The third year at Lot Whitcomb, these same teachers took the time to prepare a full day of professional development for their colleagues, not for fame, not for pay, and not because it was mandated. They shared their collective ideas and observations about newly articulated common goals, common expectations, and community successes. Increased buy-in took place in that in-between group, and the school ultimately reached a critical mass of teachers working together; disciplinary incidents plunged and academic performance rose. A new way of doing school had imbued the culture.

As a side note, the faculty book discussions and in-service presentation at Lot Whitcomb were taking place during the depths of the financial meltdown in the United States, when school budgets were shrinking, class sizes were growing, and teacher stress levels were rising commensurately. These busy teachers, in theory, had even less time and energy to do something extra under such conditions. But instead, they gave up their time to engage in what they considered interesting, meaningful collaboration with caring colleagues. Collaboration to foster the well-being of a community can build positive energy. That's permeation.

Permeating academics

Remember the student guide at Kent Denver School? In addition to his Head of School and "even" his coaches, he stated that "we talk about our goals in classes all the time." Certainly it was not all the time, and it probably was not most of his teachers, but the fact is that if these goals are important to a school, they can, and should, work their way into academics, as they did at Kent Denver. More importantly, they can work their way into academics without affecting academic rigor. Just as a math class doing statistics can use data from the school's sports program for their calculations—thus making the subject more immediate to the life of the school—so might a variety of courses refer to the school's goals for well-being/character development in study or discussions. At a school like Vohnsen Academy, a history course can examine the role of leadership, and ideally of compassionate leadership in historical events, in lieu of some other focal point. At The Corlen School, there is no reason why focus could not be put on important historical events where engaged citizenship changed the course of a nation, for the better. Selections from world-class literature can be introduced, studied, and discussed in such a way that they focus on compassion, or citizenship, or leadership, or service to others, or any of a number of other possible goals.

Permeating the culture of a school best happens, especially in academics, with the creativity of an individual school faculty and the kind of brainstorming that only they can do for their particular school. The question to grapple with is: How can we present our students with the most interesting, most appropriate academic challenges possible and, similarly, challenge their growth toward our character development goals? History classes or literature/language arts classes come first to mind for most teachers. But other than these "obvious" academic courses, other avenues toward those goals all offer possibilities. What possibilities they do offer are probably best decided by the faculty that knows the students and the school best. The same kind of brainstorming can be applied to a variety of other school initiatives or programs:

- How can our advisory program help further our goals?
- What about community service? How can our program help advance our goals?
- Coaches want winning teams, but how can they help us achieve goals that many people see as equally important, while still pushing their players toward their best possible athletic performances?

That line of questioning could go on for a variety of other programs: arts, drama, speech/debate, clubs, parent associations, and assemblies or chapel services, to name just a few. And don't forget the power that classroom management and discipline can play. As illustrated in the "bad rocket ship" model on page 48, when the discipline structure is misaligned with the school's goals, it can propel student energies off in a less than ideal direction. In some schools, the way discipline is handled actually works against the school's goals.

Many educators worry that working toward character goals might detract from academics. Two facts make such worries unwarranted. The first is the significant evidence that work to foster character development actually enhances academic performance (see, e.g., Berkowitz & Bier, 2005; Benninga et al., 2006; Weissberg et al., 2013). The issue barely merits discussion at this point. Moreover, most of the evidence pointed to in these references relates to packaged programs whose implementation required time taken from academics; the time "lost" was more than made up by the more effective learning that resulted from a healthier school culture. The second fact is that all educators, regardless of what they teach, can engage in practices every day—with no extra time, no extra effort, and no precious school monies at stake—that further both character goals and the academic goals of their own classrooms. These practices will be the focus of the Guts section of the book, to come.

What about the students?

The comments above about setting goals and integrating them into school life focused on adults, for obvious reasons. But what about students? It is, after all, they who we hope will adopt, and ultimately embody, the character goals set. If the adults at school are unable to identify the school's character goals, let's not even try to think how members of the student body would articulate what the school's hopes are. This leads to premise three, which takes permeation a step further:

We have a better chance of students being exemplars of our goals if they know what our goals are.

Harpeth Hall, in Nashville, Tennessee, is a school with a tagline at the end of its mission statement: "Inquiring minds, lives of integrity, confident leadership." One clear goal (among others) of this school for young women (grades 6 - 12) is thus to have its students graduate with confidence in their skills to lead when the call for leadership is heard. But the school's goals are more than just lines of text on the website. Aware that they have a better chance of reaching their goals when people know what they are, those in charge at Harpeth Hall have made sure the goals also have a visual presence on campus: on banners lining walkways, in words etched into the glass front of a building, and elsewhere. And clearly, at least "confident leadership" has more than just visual permeation.

On one visit to the school for a faculty workshop on advisory systems, I asked teachers to write down the two words that best marked the ideal graduate of the school. It was a relatively open-ended request and yet 75% of the faculty members present responded by writing down "confidence," "leadership," or "confident leadership." Seventy-five percent is, I reckon, more a mark of permeation than coincidence, since most Harpeth Hall teachers were present that day.

Of greater relevance to premise three is what happened that same day when I had the opportunity to engage 10 members of the senior class in one-on-one interviews. None knew that the interview was going to take place before its impromptu arrangement, and interviews took place in two or three different locations, so there was no possibility that information regarding questions was shared. To each I said "You know, during all the time you've been at this school your teachers, and the school itself, have been giving you messages about what they want you to be like when you graduate. If you had to distill that message down to just a couple of words, what two words would best describe the kind of person they want you to be?"

Eight of the ten young women focused on confidence, leadership, or confident leadership, responding with short sentences like "Well, I think they want me to be confident," or "I think they really want me to learn how to be a leader." The students I interviewed may or may not have been a representative sample of the student body, but 80% is a strong indication of a message's permeation. Harpeth Hall has a better chance of creating confident leaders if its young women know that their school wants them to develop confidence and leadership skills.

Back in Louisiana, when school recommenced at St. Martin's in the fall, the faculty addressed premise three by formally telling students about their newly envisioned goals. The message Upper School Head Scandurro gave students about the faculty's summer visioning experience: "In five years, this is going to be a student-led school." Students knew from the outset—and have been reminded throughout—that the way St. Martin's functioned as a community was their responsibility. Students shared the responsibility with their teachers, of course, and the ultimate authority for many decisions remained with the administration, but the responsibility was theirs.

It's not just high school students, by the way. Penny and Evins and Sheila Gold, with their colleagues at Isidore Newman School in New Orleans, organized the lower school (kindergarten through fifth grade) so that students saw themselves on a progressive path toward leadership development, with the expectation that they would accept leadership roles as they got into grades 4 and 5. Students understood, and could articulate, their school's goals—which collectively they referred to as the Newman Way. By the time they reached fifth grade, they grew into their responsibility to point out to younger students who might be engaging in unkind behavior in the lunch room or on the playground that "we don't do that here, it's not the Newman Way."

What the three premises say is "we have a better chance, if..."

The Kent Denver tour guide described above offered another prime example of a school that seemed to do it right in regard to premise three. None of the three premises is a guarantee that goals will be reached, of course. Students with horrible ethics can emerge from the best organized and most loving of schools, and true saints can emerge from the least organized and caring of schools. But what the three premises say is "we have a better chance, if..." And it's hard to reach goals if no one knows what they are. It's hard to reach goals if only a few people are working toward them. It's harder to get students to develop certain characteristics when we fail to let them know what those characteristics are.

As a final comment in regard to goals and sharing them with students, there is a difference between knowing goals and "having a program." It's the difference between "We use Facing History & Ourselves" or "Our elementary grades use Second Step" (both of which are great avenues for accomplishing certain goals) and "We want all our students to master the skills of regulating their emotions, being sensitive to others, and solving interpersonal conflicts." These latter three are not the names of packaged programs, but actual goals. The names of programs may be important, but it is the goals that both adults and students should be able to articulate.

Permeation is an ongoing process

Finally, the culture of a school is not built by a day of professional development or by a kick-off assembly to launch an initiative. Human beings sometimes change overnight, but rarely. Closer to our subject here, cultures never change overnight. Doing this kind of work takes commitment. Most of all it takes time. Both Lot Whitcomb and St. Martin's Episcopal School took five years to effect the changes described here. Were the results worth the work? In both cases, the answer was, and is, an emphatic yes. And there are victories along the way. Some results come quickly; but growth is sporadic, and the impression of "two steps forward, one step back" sometimes applies. In the cases of both these schools—and in others that do similar work—there was a need to revisit plans, to revise plans, to train or educate staff, to check on progress, to see what seemed to work and what did not. The work was ongoing, and it was regular. Neither school can rest on its laurels, even today. New kids come in the door, new faculty begin their careers, and old "habits" sometimes creep back, especially in times of stress. Permeation does happen, but it requires ongoing efforts.

6

Assessment

Once upon a time a school had a cheating problem. Sixteen members of the junior class were sharing information for an exam, all tapping into the same, organized, system. They got caught. With such a large number involved, the local newspaper heard about the scandal, and made the most of it. Teachers were in an uproar; something had to be done. A few of the old timers added a touch of cynicism: "You're never going to change them. Kids have been cheating for generations and they'll cheat until the end of time. Don't waste your energy."

But try they must, and try they did. Concerned teachers met, and remet, and continued to meet. They devised strategy, made plans, mapped interventions. They met with students, they crafted protocols. The school year ended, and the new one began. The teacher committee worked on into the new year. Yes, things felt better. A few students said they thought there was less cheating. It seemed like progress. And a new year turned.

Nearly three years hence, the unthinkable occurred. Five sophomores and two juniors were sharing materials for an upcoming test. Two of the boys were actually selling the materials, and had done so on previous occasions. Adults were crestfallen; except, of course, those who felt vindicated: "We told you so. They've been cheating for generations; you're not going to change anything. Where there are kids, there will always be cheaters."

The pessimists in this fictitious school were right, of course, at least if we take history into consideration. There have been cheaters at least as far back as records exist and thus, by extension, there might well be cheaters until the end of time. In another sense, however, the nay sayers were wrong with "You're not going to change anything." As the studies of Don McCabe and others tell us (see, e.g., McCabe & Treviño, 1993; Stephens & Wangaard, 2011), there is plenty of evidence that academic integrity or lack thereof is influenced by what happens at school. School efforts can make a difference.

The pessimists' attitude that nothing had changed was based solely on opinion, and in this case was contrary to fact. The tragedy in this story is that a large group of concerned, dedicated teachers put three years of blood, sweat, and tears into a cause, only to have no data to discern the possible results of their work. In fact, despite a few isolated, opinion-based comments and a general feeling that things were going better, the only hard evidence they had of anything was of failure when the second incident occurred. If they had taken the time to collect some numbers before beginning their interventions—even a simple anonymous survey—here's what they might have found around the time of the first cheating incident.
- 62% of students admitted to "cheating" on a major paper or exam in the past 12 months.
- 71% of students agreed with the statement that "cheating is not a big deal."
- 78% affirmed agreement with the statement "nearly all students in this school cheat at some time or another."

After several months of interventions to change the culture around academic integrity, had the teachers done the survey again, they might have found:
- 46% of the students admitted to cheating in the past 12 months.
- 51% agreed that "cheating is not a big deal."
- 38% endorsed the opinion that "nearly all students in this school cheat at some time or another."

Here's the graph, with the black bars representing the initial numbers—the year of the first incident—and the gray bars representing three years later. Reductions of 16 to 40 percentile points are not as stellar as this school might like, but they do indicate significant positive movement.

Structure & Guts of Character Education

	"I have cheated in the past 12 months"	"cheating is not a big deal"	"nearly all students in this school cheat at some time or another"
First Survey	62%	71%	78%
Two Years Later	46%	51%	38%

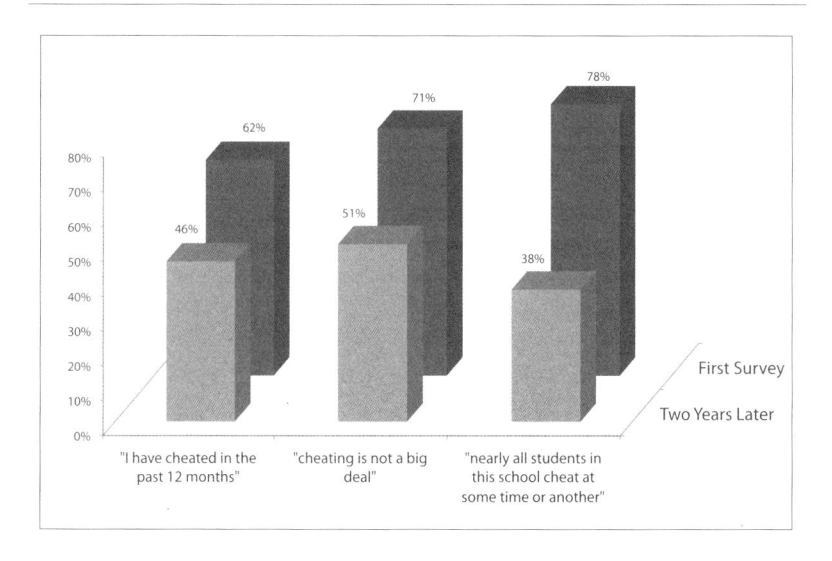

If the school had done these surveys such that students were identified by year in school, results might also have shown that cheating was diminishing in the upper grades, suggesting the adults' efforts were making a little progress year by year. In other words, survey data would not only have shown progress, it would also have given the school information regarding where that progress was being made. The numbers were lower in all three areas: student behavior, attitudes, and perception of the number of peers who were cheating. There were still far too many students who thought it was not a big deal to cheat, but school culture was heading in the right direction.

That's why data collection matters. It distinguishes between "our efforts appear to be useless," and "we're making progress." That's a big difference. Plus, lots of gradations in between those two points of failure and apparent success offer material for further investigation, and deeper understanding. Sometimes the information we collect raises more questions than it answers, but this can be helpful too.

For example, one year an elementary school at our symposium on model character development programs shared two slides of assessment data they had collected. The presenters understood the wisdom in assessment, and in their desire to be responsible educators, they took a stab at it. Coincidentally, this school was instituting a new character code. One of the things they wanted to assess was the extent to which the new code was being integrated into daily life. The assessment committee constructed a survey to look at both implementation and early permeation. Wisely, they surveyed both teachers and students. The first of the two slides illustrated teacher replies to survey items. Ninety-one percent of the teachers asserted both that "I talk about the character code in class on a daily basis" and that "Use of the character code is reflected in my language throughout the day." That is excellent information, and bodes well for success, given that so many teachers were working the code into the school day. The presenters then showed the second slide, regarding student perceptions. Only 26% of the students endorsed that "My teacher talks about the character code often."

Some observers might be amused at that disparity—91% of teachers versus 26% of students saying yes to the same phenomenon— others are shocked. Those of us at the symposium admired the presenters for their willingness to share their embarrassing discrepancy. The beauty in their survey was that at least now they have something to work with. For example, they are now in a position to ask "What can we do differently to help students recognize the new code when it comes up in class?" They might have more questions than they had previously (including whether teachers were as faithful in their efforts as the numbers suggested), but at least they have information that might help them improve their program.

Lot Whitcomb, the elementary school in chapter 2 that made such progress developing student self-management of behavior, is a public school. Because public schools are generally good about collecting data, Lot Whitcomb had lots of information at its disposal. Though there were times of frustration and disappointment, Lot Whitcomb's data allowed teachers in the school to realize that in five years of work to foster student autonomy, relationships, and competence, the number of students sent to the office had greatly decreased and the number of students suspended was cut to one-twentieth of what it had been earlier. At the same time, average percentile scores in state academic testing rose by over thirty points in math and by over forty points in reading. These results are phenomenal. Based on student attitudes and their behaviors—on the playground, in the halls, in the lunch room— teachers had a sense that they were making progress, but the numbers are so much more gratifying, and precise, than a simple "we feel like we've made progress." That's the beauty of assessment.

Ed DeRoche, at the International Center for Character Education at the University of San Diego, addresses a number of assessment strategies in his book *Evaluating Character Development* (DeRoche, 2004). DeRoche wants character educators to have an entire "toolbox" at their disposal, and to choose the instrument most appropriate for the assessment question(s) they want to answer. In some cases, doing individual interviews, holding a focus group, or collecting anecdotes might best gather the information the group wants, whereas in other scenarios those looking for information might want it to be more quantifiable, or want those supplying the information to have a sense of anonymity. In the latter cases, a survey, questionnaire, or rating scale might be preferable to interviews or focus groups. Rating scales and questionnaires also work better for larger groups. DeRoche's resource is worthwhile reading for any school wanting to explore assessment options. Some of what he includes in the book has been tested in schools; other instruments were constructed as examples only, for school teams to use as models for their own adaptation.

Others have also developed assessment aids, like the Character Education Partnership's (character.org) Evaluation Tool Kit to help schools hone their effectiveness in character-related issues, and the wide variety of scales created and offered by the Institute for Excellence and Ethics (excellenceandethics.org) to help gauge the effectiveness of interventions, or to assess general climate or culture. A number of instruments are available. Rather than focus on the specifics of the perfect tool, however, which depend so much on a school's particular assessment questions, let us stress that evaluating our efforts is essential to the structure of a responsibly-designed initiative to develop character. A couple of additional points are pertinent to this assertion.

- **Evaluation is important. Do it!**

Discuss in committee the best avenues for your school to gauge progress, and then act on the results of your discussion. What you do does not need to be perfect, but it does need to be responsible, and intentional. Attempt to collect data that will help you understand how to reach your goals more effectively, as well as how you are already being effective. I've been in too many discussions, after the kids are gone, at the last faculty meeting, where a program director raised the question "By the way, how do you feel like we've been doing with...?" The dots can be filled in with the name of a program that was at one point considered to be of sufficient importance that faculty members were asked to give their time and energies to it, but which got short shrift when dealt with in this manner at the end of the school year. If a program is important, it deserves the respect of appropriate evaluation.

- **Be intentional, even if imperfect.**

If you can get assistance from someone with test construction experience, by all means take advantage of the expertise. But in most cases, it's fine to start with the simplest methods you can devise that you feel will provide useful information. Keep it as uncomplicated as possible, but call on expertise when you feel you need it. Most simple assessment tasks of the types we are talking about, or those addressed in DeRoche's book, do not need oversight beyond the skill level that can be found in most schools. I wonder if the discrepancy in the student/teacher responses in the elementary school presentation mentioned earlier would have looked different if exactly the same wording were used in both teacher and student surveys. The teacher prompts referred to talking about the character code "on a daily basis," and reflecting the code in language "throughout the day." Students, meanwhile responded to "My teacher talks about the character code often." Indeed, the numbers might have been different with consistent wording, but no real harm was done; the school was far better off with the survey it constructed than if it had administered nothing at all.

Decide when. Most formal assessment does not need to be frequent, but frequency does depend on the information sought. Culture changes like those described earlier at St. Martin's and Lot Whitcomb took five years; a measure every year, or even two, is probably sufficient to assess progress for an issue like culture. It would be a waste of time to try to measure such large scale progress after six weeks. On the other hand, the assessment question for the elementary school symposium presenters was not "Has the character code made a difference?" At this point, it was "Are teachers doing their part to get it known?" and, "At this point is the code being noticed by students?" An early assessment is important for issues like implementation, as it is for making sure the school's goals are widely understood. For many social or emotional skills, assessment should be simpler, and sooner, than assessment of climate or culture. The main point is for those at school to put their collective minds together for a communal decision regarding when assessment is best made relative to their particular goals.

There actually should be one rule about timing. Interventions intended to produce change, especially large scale change, need a measure at the beginning, right? Otherwise, it becomes very difficult to see if progress has taken place by the end. The fictional school that started this chapter would have benefited greatly from a baseline measure regarding cheating and academic integrity. Unfortunately, it had none.

Decide why. To quote character educator Marvin Berkowitz "Whatever is assessed needs to reflect the aims of your initiative… It is essential that the measures you choose match the aims of the program" (n.d., p. 8). Like character initiatives, assessment needs to be purposeful. Don't do it unless you know why you are doing it, unless you know what information you are looking for, and unless you plan to act on meaningful results. Is the goal to notice if interventions have produced a change? Is it to discover the extent to which a specific social skill is mastered? Is it to find out how many different areas of the school (athletics, student government, the history department, etc.) are participating in advancing the school's goals? It's not fair to use resources, including (and especially) people, for assessment unless there is a clear idea regarding what information is being sought.

Decide how. Be strategic. That is, pick the best instrument or instruments you can think of, and administer it, or them, to the right people. How to assess follows from why. Whatever the question, devise the assessment to look for that particular answer. After you know why you are assessing—what you are looking for—it should be easier to discern the most direct way, how, to get that information, and whom to get it from. Make it as simple as is feasible. Then give yourself permission to stop looking for other things to measure. Don't bog your colleagues (or yourself) down with superfluous data searches.

Making assessment data more meaningful

DeRoche addresses the idea of "breadth of assessment" with the term triangulation, suggesting the use of three measures rather than single or dual sources of data" (2004, p. 9). In assessing school climate, for example, it is essential to get student input, but he suggests getting input from teachers and administrators, also, "to determine the extent to which there is congruence" (p. 9). Though the elementary school character educators with the two slides of assessment results were one data source short of triangulation, their results are a good illustration of DeRoche's point. What if their character committee had surveyed only teachers? Some might have considered the 91% figure "proof" that the new character code was becoming a part of classroom culture. On the other hand, what if they had surveyed only students? The evidence (26%) might have suggested that only one teacher in four was integrating the code into classes. There are a number of ways to interpret the discrepancy between teacher reports of their own behavior and student perceptions of teacher behavior; the truth might lie somewhere between the two, but the results do tell us that some kind of adjustment was needed in what the school was doing. Such information would never have been as clear without assessment.

Do not grade students on character

We'll close this chapter with an opinion that, though personal, follows from a certain logic. It is this: if your school's goal is for all students to develop character, do not grade students on their character. Yes, it's a temptation some of us fall into, but all the evidence suggests it's a temptation that may cause more harm than good.

Probably the most common rationale for grading character traits is "If we want to be as serious about character as we are about academics, then we should grade character." The implication is that grading something will increase its importance.

Think back on your favorite subject in high school, and on your least favorite subject. They both got graded. Did the fact of grading make you take either more seriously? By seriously, I mean that after the course was over, did you have a lot more respect for your least favorite subject? Did you start reading more books about it, and want to take additional courses to learn more? If you were one of the few people who did start to take their least favorite subject more seriously, it was probably not because it was graded, but rather because while taking it, you learned something that helped you value it more. The fact is that teachers can do things that help students take an "uninteresting" subject more seriously. But grading the subject is not one of them. This important phenomenon will be addressed in the chapter on autonomy.

A second commonly offered reason for grading character, beyond a school's hope to raise the importance of character, is that of wanting to "reward" students who do excel. Similar reasoning, with similar evidence, applies: those rewards—to be discussed in greater depth in the Guts chapter on feedback—have little meaning and may even undermine students' natural inclination to reach out for the benefit of others.

Think for a moment about the student you might identify as your least favorite example of a good citizen. If the student gets the lowest grade available possible for citizenship, almost certainly his or her first thought is not "I really want to work on my behavior so that, next time, I too can get a good grade in citizenship." Though we do not know the back story of that student's life and what led to where he or she is now, the most probable reaction is one of indifference, anger, or resentment. Indifference, anger, and resentment do not lead, usually, to good behavior, and they are not conducive to character development. In sum, a rewarding grade for citizenship, or empathy, or integrity, is a minor but relatively meaningless boost for those who excel, and an underminer of motivation for those we most want to benefit from our endeavors. The overall effect may well be negative.

Character versus behavior

As a final observation regarding the issue of grading character, let's refocus on the goal. Is it behavior change that we want, or is it character development? Grading academic courses might cause an upturn in academic behaviors in some students. Will this upturn be due to taking the subject matter seriously, or taking the power of grades seriously? Though behavior and character are related, behavior can be stimulated (modified) by rewards, threats, shame, guilt… or by an internal disposition to act for the well-being of others. It is only the latter that we call character. It is only the latter that we want. And though we cannot mandate such a disposition, there are specific, easily implemented ways that both parents and educators can foster its development. Grading is not one of them. What they are will be the focus of the second part of this book, now to come.

7

The Guts of Character Education

In an occasional workshop, usually around lunch time, a series of six or seven slides flit across on the screen. One slide shows a three layer white cake, beautifully decorated with vanilla frosting; it is followed by a richly dark German chocolate cake, and then by a plate of brownies, a pile of hot-out-of-the-oven chocolate chip cookies, a slide or two of other layer cakes with different kinds of frosting, and a pineapple upside down cake with fresh fruit arranged on the top. The question that follows is "what do all these slides have in common?"

The artistic presentation of the desserts is what makes them stand out, of course. Indeed, what the viewer notices is the presentation, and presentation is the name of the game at the pastry shop. The point of the slides, however, is what holds them together. Beyond the frills of fruit, powdered sugar, and icing, the substance of what we are looking at is three primary ingredients: flour, butter, and sugar. Looking through the shop window, we don't usually focus on the basics. But think about what goes on in the back of the store: if you own that bakery and you haven't mastered flour, butter, and sugar, your business is in trouble.

Another slide occasionally used in workshops is cluttered with educational terms current in good schools today. Clutter refers to the arrangement, not to what the terms stand for. What all those items on the slide have in common is that, to the best of my recollection, none of them existed as an important educational idea when I began my teaching career. Some of the terms and the practices they refer to were probably in use, but as far as I know they were not current practice in schools.

> brain-based learning   advisory group
> value of the month   STEM   honors courses
> diversity coordinator   multiple intelligences
> appreciative inquiry   service learning   self-study
> honor council   media literacy
> flipped classroom   resilience   core values
> self-determination theory   common core
> global curriculum   mentorship program
> collaborative learning   differentiated instruction
> digital literacy
> challenge course   mission statement
> interim courses   grit   executive functioning
> block scheduling   global learning
> response to intervention   curriculum mapping
> understanding by design   formative assessment

The slide in question is "built" such that the words fade away, to the point where all that remains is "self-determination theory" in the center. I'll be among the first to admit the power and importance of a number of the concepts represented on that slide—design thinking, service learning, media literacy to name just a few—but the point of the second half of this book, and of *Breaking into the Heart of Character* that preceded it, is that the three components of self-determination theory—autonomy, relationships, and competence—are the butter, the flour, and the sugar of good educational practice, and of good character education practice. Here's why: in contrast to all those other terms, these three concepts, which are the focus of the next three chapters, are human needs. The other items on the slide are interesting—sometimes good, sometimes even brilliant—educational concepts or strategies, but the three aspects of self-determination theory are *essential* for the kind of psychological functioning and internal motivation that high quality education and character development require. Stated another way, if a school dropped its media literacy program, its honor council, and even its community service program (which I hope never happens), high quality education could continue. But envision a school where students feel like they have no power, no support, and few of the skills they need for life; it's not going to be a happy, let alone productive, place for anyone.

Structure & Guts of Character Education

So we're going to switch metaphors for the second part of this book. The lenses, I hope, worked well for envisioning goals for character development. Structure helps guide practice. In this second part we're going to focus on the practice; more specifically, we are going to focus on what, deep inside, helps practice be successful. It's not showy work, but it's critical. Moreover, what is being dealt with as "guts" here is not a program for character development. The 33 numbers on the Berkowitz and Bier chart from chapter four represent programs, and what Weissberg, Goren, Domitrovich, and Dusenbury (2013) discuss in the CASEL Guide is programs, as are the interventions reviewed by the Institute for Educational Sciences at the U.S. Department of Education's What Works Clearinghouse (http://ies.ed.gov/ncee/wwc/document.aspx?sid=23). Even the home grown set of activities the talented staff at your school might have conceived to foster social, emotional, and moral growth can be considered a program. But the skills taught, the activities engaged in, and the knowledge learned in these programs—all tremendously important—are like the coloring and flavoring and layering, and even the added ingredients that distinguish cookies from brownies, or German chocolate from devil's food. They may all be beautiful (or not), and many of them have been shown to be effective. But if the three components addressed in the next three chapters are not folded into the mix, all the pink frosting in the world will not save the bakery.

These chapters discuss autonomy support, relatedness, and competence as they apply to school life. Whereas the material presented in *Breaking into the Heart of Character* addressed the roles that autonomy, relatedness, and competence play in both academic motivation and character development, the shorter presentation here addresses primarily the latter. It is my contention that the best structured character development program in the world—including the best of the programs reviewed by those mentioned on the previous page, and indeed any program, even, that follows to the letter the goal-identification, permeation, and assessment recommendations made in the first half of this book—is doomed to failure without careful attention to the guts of the second half.

8

Autonomy

Choice, Voice, Structure, Relevance

When we think about students of character, without exception we want that character to come from within. We want any action—an apology, an expression of kindness, a manifestation of integrity—to be performed not because someone demanded it, not because someone is watching, but because the action emerges from the very core of the individual, because it feels "right." In other words, we want the action to be autonomous.

Autonomous action is not just an item on adults' wish lists, however. Autonomy is a human need. It is a need that every student and every teacher who walks through the school door has to have filled if "best possible performance" is the goal. As we'll see shortly, a sense of autonomy affects not just the quality of one's performance, it affects emotional health and the quality of social interactions, in addition to motivation, self-regulation, and well-being. As we'll also see, there are specific actions adults can take that foster autonomy. Let's preface what these things are by being clear about what autonomy is, and is not.

What is autonomy?

Many people see autonomy as a synonym for independence, for freedom from constraint, for doing whatever one wants to do. Self-determination theory looks at autonomy differently, with a focus on two primary characteristics. The aspect of freedom certainly is there, as one of these characteristics is volition: how much control one has over an action, how freely it is performed. Autonomy technically means "self-rule," implying that one is regulating one's own behavior and experience, and thus that one is in control of both initiating an action and the direction in which it proceeds (Ryan & Powelson, 1991). When actions are intrinsically motivated, they are highly volitional: we want to engage in them; involvement is enjoyment. But most of what needs to be done at school is far from intrinsically motivated. Teachers can offer a small measure of freedom by using inviting language (rather than commanding or controlling language) because inviting language offers students a measure of choice and control. On the whole, though, offering choice can only do so much. That's where the other characteristic comes into play.

This second aspect of autonomy, self-endorsement, pertains to the extent to which we "buy into" activities, the extent to which we see their worth (Ryan et al., 2008, p. 158; see also Ryan & Deci, 1990, 2000; Deci et al,. 1991). Understanding how to increase "buy in" is a critical factor for educators (and for parents), because knowledge of how to do so opens up ways of teaching and interacting that foster greater motivation (both for academics and for social behavior—and greater well-being). It's a beautiful possibility, with much to say about the science and the art of education. Let's use the motivation rings from the graphic in *Breaking into the Heart of Character* as an illustration.

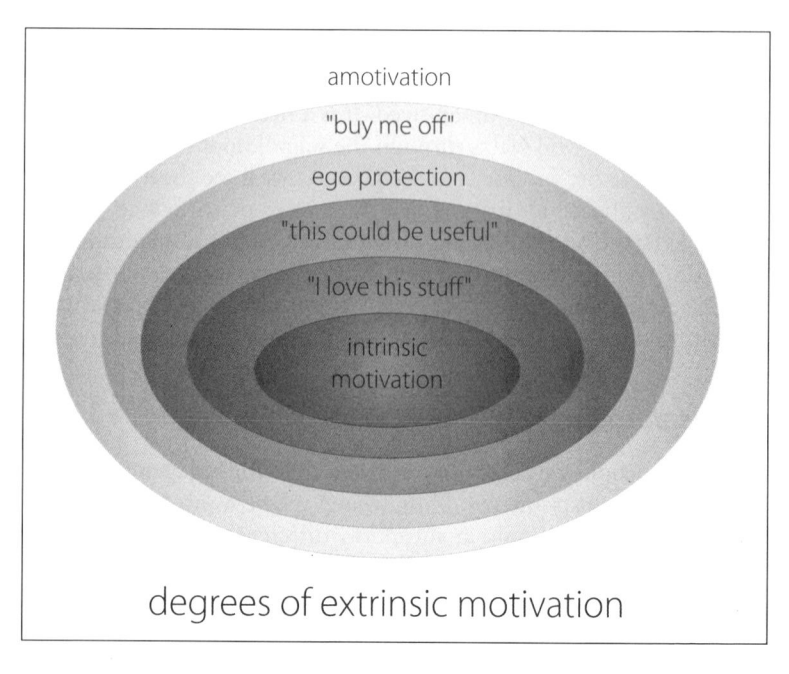

amotivation
"buy me off"
ego protection
"this could be useful"
"I love this stuff"
intrinsic motivation

degrees of extrinsic motivation

Structure & Guts of Character Education

At the very center of this illustration is a small core where intrinsic motivation resides, where actions are performed for the pure joy of it. The experience of spending time with things we're intrinsically motivated for, especially if they challenge us appropriately, is what the concept of "flow" is all about. We can lose all track of what is happening around us. Unfortunately we really don't get to spend much time at the center of the diagram. Most of school happens in rings outside the intrinsic core—sometimes far outside.

Outside the intrinsic center are rings that represent varying degrees of extrinsic motivation. The ring farthest from the center is what is referred to as extrinsically regulated motivation. Basically, people in this outer ring have very little interest in—very little autonomous motivation for—the activity in question. People engage in activities "out here" primarily because of the rewards involved (money, prizes, stickers, whatever) or to avoid negative consequences. That is why it is labeled "buy me off" in the illustration. The boy doing community service whose primary focus is fulfilling a requirement or avoiding being hassled by adults is working in this ring. The girl who apologizes because the apology was mandated after she angrily cursed in the hallway is, similarly, externally regulated. There's no real desire; the only thing really "self-endorsed" here is getting past the unpleasantness as quickly as possible.

In a ring just inside "buy me off" is a degree of motivation that represents a tiny bit more personal value and commitment—though perhaps not much. In this ring, people are motivated because their egos push them or pull them to avoid feelings of shame or guilt, or to shore up a less-than-secure sense of self. Academically, students motivated in this ring are not truly interested in the subject matter. Rather, they study to maintain self-esteem or to avoid feeling incompetent or ashamed. Notice that there is not much autonomy here, but there is a little. It is the student who is choosing the action—so volition is there—but there is not much buy in or value for the academic subject itself.

Giving a donation to a worthy cause in this "ego" ring might mean that the donation is motivated by a desire not to feel guilty. Picking up trash left behind by other students in the cafeteria could be done in a variety of rings. If a student picks it up because doing so momentarily allows him to feel superior to those who made the mess, the motivation probably fits at this "ego-protection/ego enhancement" level. If, on the other hand, the student focused not on his own feelings but on the fact that his class—and thus he, too—could get detention for the mess, then the motivation falls into the outermost ring of rewards and punishment.

The next ring, a little closer to the center, represents a level we have referred to as "this could be useful." As the name suggests, what we're doing in this ring does not completely feel like "us," but we can see its possible value. At this level, for example, the student's motivation for working on Habitat for Humanity's house might be because she sees it as great training for something she might want to do later in life. The aspiring actor who wants to work at the retirement center to get a sense of how old people talk, move, and interact is indeed motivated to engage in the service project, but it's a very different level of motivation from the student who has learned to value the work and its purpose.

A couple of my long-time colleagues have a daughter who is an avid reader, and she loves certain areas of American literature. I don't know if Kellin's reading is purely intrinsic, or if it is integrated, but it is one or the other. She derives great enjoyment from literature, and thus her motivation for reading certain genres and certain authors is very close to the center of the motivation chart. At one period shortly after college, Wallace Stegner was one of Kellin's favorite writers.

Among the acquaintances of Kellin's friends was a guy—Jason—who took an interest in Kellin and hoped he could get himself noticed. So he followed Kellin's social media posts, which included references to her recent reading. Subsequently, or we might say consequently, Jason, too, became motivated to read Wallace Stegner. Earlier, reading Stegner was something Jason might have done if it was assigned, but let's observe that after meeting Kellin and learning of her reading interests, Jason realized that "Wallace Stegner could be useful." So the ring of his motivation took a step closer to the center. As it happened, the next time he was in Kellin's presence, a well-placed comment like "Oh, I was reading *Crossing to Safety* the other day, and there's this beautiful passage..." tended to be of much utility for Jason. A couple of Stegner novels later, they were engaged.

One ring remains in the self-determination theory schematic. The ring closest to the center is one that self-determination scholars refer to as integrated motivation: integrated, because we feel that these activities represent what we value to such a high degree that they are integral to our sense of self. Many teachers feel this way about their profession. Doing what they do is hard, of course, but for many there is such joy in the interactions they have with colleagues and students, and such fulfillment in working with subject matter they love and in seeing students make progress, that the work is a rich, meaningful, highly valued and highly satisfying experience. Many students find themselves motivated for certain academic subjects at this level, also, or for community service experiences. Building a house with Habitat for Humanity or tutoring at a local elementary school is not necessarily something some students would do for the pure intrinsic enjoyment of it, and yet there is a deep fulfillment, interest, and personal involvement in what they are doing.

Let's stop for a moment and go back to a statement made earlier, about the two primary components of autonomy. The first component entailed how freely and willingly an act is performed. The trash picked up to avoid detention was not done with much heart, but the student was not forced to do it, either. The same was probably true of the donation to charity, assuming there was no external pressure. So to a certain extent, volition was present, but it's obvious that something is still missing. On the other hand, little volition was present when the girl was mandated to apologize for her language in the hallway; she pretty much had to do it.

The second aspect of autonomy was that of self-endorsement of activities, of how much an individual values them. Notice that, in the outer rings, the action is not really valued; it is performed primarily for some reason other than because the student sees it as important. Actions from that outermost ring that we engage in to avoid hassles (e.g., the trash picked up in the cafeteria) or to get rewards, are typically valued very little by the person "motivated" to perform them. In the ego-protection ring a little closer to the center, where actions are done to keep from feeling bad, or to prop up self-esteem, they do not tend to be valued highly either. Thus, even though there is some autonomy, the degree of autonomy is low, because even if no one explicitly mandated the action, there were "external" forces that affected its getting done.

Starting with the "this could be useful" ring, we begin to buy into the action because it is seen as helpful in some way, because we start to identify with the action's value or utility. Because we are more personally motivated to engage, because the action feels more "ours," we feel more autonomy in performing it. By extension, the innermost ring is a level with a very high degree of autonomy. When we truly value something, we tend to do it with great willingness; we often look forward to engaging. Actions motivated at these inner levels feel more integral to who we truly are, and are performed with a great degree of psychological ease.

Adults can influence motivation

One of the beauties of self-determination theory is its findings that adults, through the ways they interact with young people, can influence students' growth inward, from an outer ring to one closer to the center. Not only do the inner rings feel much more "right" than the outer rings, but we now have decades of research—study after study, one adding to the evidence of its predecessors—illustrating autonomy's whats, whys, and hows, and showing that human beings on four different continents respond similarly when needs for autonomy are filled (see, e.g., Ryan & Deci, 2000a, 2000b; Reeve et al., 2002; Reeve, 2006, 2009). Time after time, these studies tell us that the closer we get to intrinsic motivation, the faster we learn material, the longer we remember it, the deeper we learn concepts, the greater sense of well-being we experience, the more creativity is enhanced, and—for those interested in "grit"—the more students tend to persist and persevere in the matter at hand (see e.g., Buff et. al., 2011; but also Reeve, 2006, 2009; Grolnick & Ryan, 1987; Ryan & Deci, 2000b; Ryan et al., 2008). More central to the topic of this book, we know that the closer we move toward intrinsic motivation, the stronger our social and emotional health, and the better our chances of feeling like acting prosocially—to foster the well-being of others (Gagné, 2003, Weinstein & Ryan, 2010).

What we address in the next section, then, is the process of "internalization"; it happens that, without great time or effort—but with a little intentional care—we are able to help students "integrate" the meaningful work that takes place at school. *Internalization* refers to the process of comprehending the value of something, of moving it from the point where it is "regulated" by forces outside to the point where it becomes more central to the individual. The term *integration* refers not just to grasping meaning, but to making an activity or subject matter more personally relevant. The goal is for students, then, is integration: "to transform more fully the regulation into their own, so that it will emanate from their sense of self" (Ryan & Deci 2000a, p. 60).

How do we foster autonomy?

Let's now look at four key strategies that lie at the heart of fostering autonomy: choice, voice, structure, and relevance. These are strategies that help, each in its own way, catalyze movement closer to the center. The most amazing thing about these four strategies is that every one of them can be employed by adults, regardless of what they teach (or even if they are not teachers), regardless of the age of their students, and regardless of whether it's a Monday in September or a Thursday in April. All four strategies can be used in just about every class, just about every day. They do not take any extra time, and they do not cost any extra money. But the benefits are manifold.

Choice

Except on rare occasions, most of us prefer the *option* to do something over a *command*. The more freedom we have in what we do, the better we feel about doing it. Okay, the fact is that we have no choice about lots of what happens at school. Both teachers and students have to show up, and they have to be there by a certain time. Most teachers have to teach the subjects they are assigned, and students have to be in the grade, and take the courses, that the school requires. Students have to do homework, too. However, within the structure imposed by those circumstances, a wide variety of choices can still be possible. The more choice teachers feel their school gives them over these circumstances, the more deeply engaged they tend to be with their work. The more control teachers can pass to their students and the more choices they can offer within the normal constraints of class structure, the more deeply their students tend to engage with their work, too; and the more sincerely and positively students engage with adults and peers (Ryan & Deci, 2000a).

Since nearly all schools have some kind of community service program, let's take service as a non-academic example. What is mandated, and what is left to student autonomy? In some schools, all students are required to participate in community service. In some of those schools, just doing some kind of community service fulfills the requirement; other schools actually mandate the number of hours that need to be fulfilled. In some schools, students get to pick how their service time will be spent. In others, students get to pick, but only from a certain number of options; in still others, students are informed that "this is what we're doing."

Before we go further, let's remember the first element from the Structure part of this book: goals. How the school approaches community service might depend on what its goals are, what its reason for having a service program is in the first place. In most schools the program probably exists because the school wants kids to develop the skills, and the will, to minister to the well-being needs of the community around them. In the context of this chapter on autonomy, what that means is that the school hopes its students will develop an inner (i.e., autonomous) desire to work for the well-being of others, so that later in life those students will continue to be sensitive to the needs of others; they will be sensitive to the needs of others not because someone is forcing it, not because they want to avoid feeling guilty, and not even because "doing service could be useful in achieving my personal goals," but ideally because "I value the well-being of others, and when I see something that I can do that might foster greater well-being in my community, I want to help."

Self-determination theory posits that the more choice we have, the better the chances of autonomous, "innermost circle" motivation. Of course, other factors come into play, but on the simplest level, the school where service is recommended and encouraged will have a better chance of fostering this autonomous attitude toward service than the school where students have 1) no choice about doing service, 2) no choice about how much service they do, and 3) no choice about what kind of service they render. Those are the basic, inescapable facts. This is not necessarily saying that mandatory service has to be eliminated; there are even ways that it might be beneficial, meaning a feasible way to reach some of the school's goals. Sometimes there are few options for the way students do service (age restrictions, for example). If so, it is helpful if students understand why only one kind of service is available. But if a variety of options exist regarding how students can help with a project, students' inner appreciation of the value of service will be more readily enhanced if they have a choice than if they are assigned to a task. Assigning is administratively easier, but choice is educationally sounder, if valuing service is the goal. In the final analysis, much depends on how the mandatory aspects are dealt with, and the following three strategies—voice, relevance, and structure—might help alleviate the obligatory feeling some students have regarding an activity that adults feel needs to be compulsory.

Voice

Like choice, voice also concerns freedom. It concerns how restricted or unrestricted students feel with their opinions, whether they feel they can express their ideas and still be respected (and accepted) after what they've said. Some teachers bristle at the idea of free expression, but let's be clear: voice does not mean "say whatever you want, whenever you want, however you want." Living together—especially when the ultimate lens of focus is the well-being of those around us—implies respect, implies the structure of appropriate time and place, implies a benevolent motive, and also implies that what is being said is being said from the heart.

For a practical example of voice, let's go back to the girl who was made to apologize for her infraction. Let's assume that she had cursed in the hallway, that her cursing was flamboyantly executed, and that the chair and vice chair of the parent association happened to be visiting that day and were unfortunately within easy earshot. First of all, using "voice" the way this girl did is not what we're talking about here. Voice refers primarily to how safe a person feels expressing opinions that are authentically held.

The teacher or administrator dealing with the flamboyant curser could begin to address the situation via careful listening to the girl's perspective regarding the scenario. The adult may or may not agree with the student's perspective, that's not the point. The point is that the interaction began with the student feeling listened to. Even if the listening was by an adult who ended up disagreeing with the account, the power of voice is that the student got a genuine chance to exercise it.

A second way to foster voice might include asking the student for suggestions regarding how to resolve the situation. The student might claim that there is no need to resolve anything, it's already over and done with; the adult probably would not agree. I wouldn't. I would like her to apologize, sincerely and formally, to the PTA officers. But my agreement or lack thereof is irrelevant to the issue of voice here; what is relevant is the student's perception that I genuinely sought her input regarding this issue, and that I listened respectfully.

There is an equal chance that the student might suggest some kind of resolution via a suggestion that is inappropriate given the circumstances, or does not go far enough ("I should go home and talk to my mom about what I said" or "I should check a book out of the library about swearing" or "I should be more careful next time"). On rare occasions, a student will suggest something that far exceeds the severity of what the adult would think appropriate ("I should get suspended for a week," or "I should have to wear duct tape over my mouth for the next three days"). In all of these instances, voice can still be honored, and then an amended recommendation can be introduced by the adult. An amended resolution to the issue is much easier to accept after one feels listened to sincerely. More importantly, the ability to exercise voice before deciding on a resolution supports the student's sense of autonomy, and thus the student's growth.

On equally rare occasions, a student might suggest something that an adult would have wanted to mandate, like "I should write a letter of apology to those ladies, telling them what happened, that I am sorry, and I will work harder to watch my language." There is far more power for growth when a course of action is autonomously selected and executed than otherwise. Back to the goals: if the goal is to demonstrate to the PTA chairs that "at this school, we don't tolerate rude behavior," it matters little whether the letter is mandated or volunteered. However, if the goal is catalyzing moral growth in the student, then the letter volunteered by the student, or the letter suggested by the adult after the student did not consider it, or even a letter mandated by the adult but mandated only after the student feels respectfully listened to, does more to internalize motivation than the immediate mandate of a formal apology. Whether the consequences of this incident foster social and moral development or not—whether they internalize motivation or not—lies to a certain degree in the consequences themselves, and to a far greater degree in the way they were reached.

A number of studies have looked at autonomy where voice was one of the variables (e.g., Vansteenkiste et al., 2012; Assor et al., 2002). In one of these (Assor et al., 2002) researchers looked at teacher behaviors that supported, or suppressed, autonomy, in over 800 students, some from grades 3-5, and others in grades 6-8. Students in both age groups had similar reactions to teacher behaviors. One of two factors that most moved the needle regarding student engagement in learning was voice, in this case whether students felt they were allowed to express a negative opinion regarding the class or the teacher. The variables were assessed via student reactions to statements like "the teacher acts in a vindictive way toward students who oppose her opinions," and "the teacher is willing to listen only to opinions that fit her opinion." Rare is the teacher who wants to hear student opinions that contradict his or her own, and especially if that student's feelings seem to be shared by others. Powerful, though, is the teacher who is able to listen to student frustration or disagreement, who tries to see the frustration from the student's point of view, and who then accepts what is expressed (and the student), not as a personal affront but rather as the reality of an individual struggling to understand and grow into a competent, self-regulated human being.

Structure

Autonomy support is frequently, but erroneously, interpreted as getting rid of structure. That is far from the case. Not only are the two completely compatible, but structure and support for autonomy actually complement one another in ways that are beneficial to academic and sociomoral progress. What is destructive are the opposites of autonomy support and structure, meaning chaos or lack of clarity, and a style of teaching (or parenting) that is perceived as controlling or manipulative (Reeve, 2006, p. 231-232).

In an educational context, Reeve (2006) defines structure as teachers "communicating clearly what they expect students to do to achieve academic goals" (pp. 231-232). For academic work in the classroom, that concerns explanations of what the learning activity involves, what it means to "master" the material, the time frame available to work on projects, and how students are expected to work together, among other things. For behavioral interactions, structure can also mean clarity on what behaviors are expected and appropriate, when certain behaviors may not be permitted (even if they are permitted at other times), where it is appropriate, or inappropriate, to engage in certain behaviors, and so forth. Reeve and Halusic (2009) add two other adult behaviors that support autonomy, in addition to clear expectations: guidance for students' activity, and constructive feedback (p. 148). More will be said about feedback in two chapters to come, in regard to competence.

When presented the right way, structure can be liberating, because the parameters it sets up means students do not have to waste time or energy trying to discover where they are, what they are supposed to be doing, and how. My daughter recently engaged her elementary school students in a practice test for the state's assessment of written language. When students discovered, after the practice session, that they had been writing more than the state really required, she claimed she could see the tension level in the classroom dissipate. One element of structure for that assignment was length. Knowing the parameters of what was expected gave students more control, because they knew better what to aim for. It also fostered students' sense of competence. The realization of the length element was accompanied by comments like "Oh, that's easy. We can do that!"

How structure is presented matters greatly, though. Actually, how structure is presented is crucial. It can be presented in a controlling fashion, where students perceive it as mandated by adult whims, possibly to make students' lives miserable; or it can be presented in an informational and more inviting fashion, accompanied by a rationale regarding why certain boundaries or parameters are important. It is this "interpersonal context" (Deci et al., 2001, p. 4) that influences how students perceive expectations, and their perceptions do affect the development of both autonomy and competence. Presenting structure along with rationale is covered in part in our next subtopic, relevance.

Maarten Vansteenkiste and colleagues (2012) did a study of structure and autonomy that involved over 1000 Belgian students in grades 7 through 12. Part of the procedure looked at student perceptions of their teachers and whether the teachers made expectations clear or left them unclear. Another variable considered whether teachers supported student autonomy by offering explanations in an informational way, or whether they tended to use a more controlling style (e.g., threatening punishment for tasks not completed). The students who made the most progress, both academically and socially, were those whose teachers used both structure, via clear expectations regarding the task and its parameters, and autonomy support via helping students value tasks through understanding their importance. These students reported the most autonomous motivation for studying, they devised a greater number of learning strategies, and they had fewer behavioral problems both at school (e.g., skipping classes) and outside school (e.g., drug use). As should be expected, the students who had teachers who supported autonomy but were weak on providing structure, and those who provided structure but with little explanation regarding why the structure was important, had students who took less control of their learning and had more problem behaviors. Finally, at the bottom of the list with the greatest number of behavior problems and the least self-regulated learning, were the students who perceived their teachers to be weak both in providing structure and in supporting autonomy.

Similar and related findings have resulted in studies by Jang et al. (2010) in Korea, and by Melanie Farkas and Wendy Grolnick (2010) in the United States. In their review of structure and recommendations to parents for balancing autonomy and structure, Farkas and Grolnick (2010) focused on six primary suggestions as leading to the best results:
1) set clear and consistent rules
2) use clearly conveyed and consistent consequences for actions
3) give task-focused informational feedback (for more on this, see chapter 11 of this book, and Streight, 2015, pp. 66-69)
4) offer children ample opportunities to meet expectations
5) explain the reasons for rules and expectations, and
6) use authority—meaning exert power when needed—but use it appropriately (pp. 268-269).

The bottom line is that "the essence of autonomy enhancement is not minimization of the educator's presence, but making the educator's presence useful for the student who strives to formulate and realize personal goals and interests" (Assor et al., 2002, p. 273). Structure, set up in an autonomy-supportive fashion, is a significant piece of how an "educator's presence" can be useful. Much utility also comes from the fourth of the four strategies, making the material as relevant as possible to students' lives.

Relevance

Richard Ryan and Edward Deci assert that you can never really make an action autonomous unless you "grasp its meaning and worth" (2000a, p. 64).

As noted in the discussion of volition, students have no choice about much of what happens at school. Offering choice, when it is possible to do so, is thus helpful because to a certain extent choice can diminish the obligatory feeling of mandated action. In the same vein, honoring voice can soften the feel of environments and tasks that cannot allow lots of freedom, because the human support diminishes pressure and thus allows one's thoughts or opinions to feel freer. Perhaps the most effective strategy to help fill the autonomy need is fostering relevance, however. Explanatory rationale, as the strategy is also called, means providing a reason why something might be of value. It aims to increase the "meaning and worth" of an activity or field of knowledge. When we become aware of meaning and worth, our awareness makes it easier to accept an activity as something we can buy into, something we can "own"; thus we engage more freely in it.

In one study, the importance of relevance became so salient that it affected the report's title: Choice Is Good, But Relevance Is Excellent (Assor et al., 2002). This study was referred to earlier, when voice was singled out as "One of two factors that most moved the needle regarding student engagement in learning" (p. 86). Helping students understand why something could be meaningful to their lives was the other, and even more salient, factor.

The power of relevance becomes clearer if we refer back to the rings of extrinsic motivation. Remember that the student at that outside ring had so little interest that motivation took place primarily through the enticement of rewards, or the threat of punishment. Similarly, students motivated at the ego protection or ego enhancement level act primarily for self-centered concerns. Starting at the level of identified motivation, however, the individual sees some utility in an action—it becomes a little more meaningful—so the action is performed more willingly.

At the innermost ring is where the greatest interest can be seen because that is where the greatest value resides. It is thus here that actions are performed most willingly. The student passionate about the environment does not need to be dragged to the outing to clean up a stream bed, or to pick up trash in the forest, or even to take the empty soda can home to recycle it properly. The avid fisherman might participate in the same stream cleanup, but possibly for a more utilitarian reason. So it follows that after students see and understand how something might be relevant to what they value, they might buy into it more deeply and thus engage in it more willingly (Deci et al., 1991). This is the purpose of an "explanatory rationale."

An explanatory rationale attempts to link an activity or field of information to a person's interests. This helps bring meaningfulness to light. At the simplest level, the following might work as explanatory rationales for why younger students should be nice to others:
- If you are nice to him, he might be more willing to share his toys.
- If you want other kids to be nice to you, you need to be nice to them.
- Maybe he treats you that way because he thinks you don't like him. If you found a way to assure him that you have no bad feelings toward him, things might turn around.

Some explanatory rationales are more effective than others, and there is maybe more art than science involved. How an explanatory rationale is worded depends on the age of the child, the mental state of the child, the motivational level of the child—rewards and punishments versus ego-enhancement, for example—and probably a host of other factors.

For the unhappy student with no motivation for community service, a scatter blast might work best: "Look, I understand that you don't like this, but service is something we want students to do because we want our graduates to be sensitive to the needs of our community. At least we hope that kids will understand, and appreciate, their community better. Maybe some of the activities in our service projects can even teach skills for later life, or help kids get to know some fascinating human beings outside the school."

This hodgepodge actually heads off in a number of different directions, hoping that something in there might "stick" for a student we don't know that well. The last resort, to be avoided unless nothing else seems to work, might be a rationale that some see as "externally regulated," but others might take as utilitarian: "You know, you're never going to get a high school diploma from this school unless you do this." At least the high school diploma, too, is a rationale, and thus more helpful than the more controlling "Tough, do it anyway." But accompany that externally regulated reason with an invitation into the more central rings; add something like "I'm hoping you'll feel better about it after you do something that other people really need."

Researchers have looked at the specific role that providing a rationale plays in engagement and motivation. In the 1990s, Edward Deci and colleagues (1994) got participants to press a space bar on a keyboard whenever a light appeared on their computer screen. Some of the participants were given no reason for the procedure, and others were told that air traffic controllers were given this task as part of their training because it enhanced their concentration and their abilities to catch certain signals. Participants who were given the rationale did report seeing the task as more important, and stuck to it longer.

A few years later, Johnmarshall Reeve and colleagues (2002) followed up Deci's work in two different studies, by presenting college students with a lesson in conversational Chinese. The lesson was constructed to be both uninteresting (like pressing the space bar) and of only minimal relevance to students' daily lives. In the experiment, one group of students was not offered any rationale for why they should put effort into the lesson; they just got the lesson and were instructed to do it. The remaining students were divided into three groups, and each group was offered a different rationale for "trying hard." The three rationales represented different rings in the motivation chart: the external regulation group was asked to try hard because they were going to be tested to see how well they had studied the information. The introjected, ego-related ring was represented by students—all of whom were majoring in education—being told that "this is what today's classroom teacher should do; it's what a good teacher ought to want to do." The rationale for the third group aimed more at getting students to identify with the worth of the lesson; they were told it offered "the opportunity to gain a skill that will be very handy when you are a classroom teacher." Another variable in the experiment looked at the difference between offering the rationale in an inviting fashion, or in a more authoritarian, commanding fashion. Aside from the already-documented finding that an explanatory rationale facilitates the internalization of motivation, what is important from the results of these studies is 1) that the rationale closest to the center of the rings ("this skill will come in handy later, when you teach") was more effective than the other two rationales, and 2) that the autonomy-supportive, rather than controlling, language had a measurable positive effect.

How teachers can avoid killing motivation

Of the three factors that begin the Guts part of this book—autonomy, relatedness, and competence—the evidence is strong that autonomy is the most salient factor when it comes to motivation. The others are essential, but autonomy stands out. Indeed, "self-determination" is a synonym for autonomy. It might be fitting, then, to close the chapter with a few well-documented adult behaviors known to kill autonomy and thus undermine motivation, and a strong plea for adults to avoid them whenever possible. Only a few references are listed here, but all the strategies noted are copiously documented in educational, psychological, developmental literature (see especially Koestner et al., 1984; Deci et al., 1991, 2001).

Avoid commands; invitations and suggestions work better

Like adults, students respond more positively to invitations and suggestions than to commands. Commands are intended to remove autonomy. Controlling language thus undermines both motivation and one's sense of well-being; inviting language from a teacher leaves some autonomy in the student's hands, and thus fosters motivation. And it's not just the fact of a command, of course. Tone of voice can be even more powerful than content. As we know, it is possible to make a suggestion that is interpreted as a command. What matters is the way the command—or the invitation or suggestion—is perceived.

Help only as much as needed, as little as possible.

An action is autonomous when we feel like we are in control of both initiating it and governing its direction (Ryan & Powelson, 1991). The teacher, the tutor, or the well-meaning parent can actually be detrimental to a child's motivation and well-being by giving too many hints about the right answer, or by doing too much of the work for a child. If an assignment gets completed, or an act of charity is performed, what is accomplished is nearly meaningless to the child unless the child feels like he or she is the one responsible for performing the act.

Eliminate rewards if they are expected and tangible

"Tangible rewards" means stickers, wristbands, stars, certificates, money, pizza, parties, extra recess, all that stuff. What happens when a reward becomes tangible and expected is that, as much as we like the reward, we feel we are being manipulated. A teacher's promise of a reward is an attempt by the teacher to influence behavior. It thus diminishes the student's perception of being in control, as well as the ability to choose to do something because it is valued. It also suggests, in some cases, that the action performed is not worthwhile in itself. The reason for good behavior in the classroom should be because good behavior makes it easier for all of us to accomplish our goals, or it helps members of the class focus on their learning. If the reason for good behavior is so we can have extra recess, the extra recess suggests that good behavior is not of value in itself.

Note, extra recess after a day of good work is not detrimental. It becomes detrimental when students start expecting the extra recess, which happens if teachers make an "if...then" deal with students, or if a teacher gives extra recess so often that students begin to count on it in exchange for doing what the teacher wants. The fact that expected tangible rewards undermine even motivation for prosocial behaviors—helping others—has been documented in children as young as 20 months old (Warneken & Tomasello, 2008).

Eliminate pressured evaluations, threats of tests

In some classrooms, "the test" becomes the focus of everyone's attention. When evaluations are emphasized, they undermine not only intrinsic motivation, but also conceptual learning and creativity (see Deci et al., 1991; Grolnick & Ryan, 1987; and, in regard to the same findings in Japan, Kage & Namiki, 1990). What is to be noted here is not that evaluations or tests are destructive. "Doing school" without evaluations is irresponsible and probably far less productive. What is damaging is when evaluations or tests are held over our heads, when they become attempts to control our behavior, as exemplified by teacher comments like "Remember, this is going to be on the test," or "Don't forget, this counts for a quarter of your grade."

The same reasoning applies to discussion about grades. If students perceive grades as a teacher's best estimate of their educational progress, then they may be helpful. If, on the other hand, students perceive grades as carrots and sticks—tools their teachers use to goad them into doing work—then the goading practice is detrimental to the development of autonomy, and thus to both motivation and well-being. If student growth is the school's goal, the pressure should be for academic and social responsibility, not for points or grades.

Threats are in a category by themselves. They sometimes work to control behavior, but the discussion of autonomy above, and relatedness now to come, suggests they are counterproductive in developing character.

9

Relatedness

Diana Baumrind has been studying parents and their interactions with children for a half century, with research that has led to the identification of four styles of parenting now widely accepted. The styles—unengaged parenting, permissive parenting, authoritarian parenting, and authoritative parenting—differ from one another along two axes, one being how nurturing, how loving, how responsive parents are to kids' needs; and the other, how demanding parents are. Demandingness in this context refers to the expectations parents have of their children, how these expectations are communicated, and how parents follow up to see if their expectations are being met or being worked toward (Baumrind, 1991a, 1991b, 2008).

Over the years, Baumrind's team at the University of California at Berkeley has been able to follow the growth of scores of children, and thus to see the effects that parenting styles have. Parents who fit into Baumrind's *unengaged* category typically have little to do with their children in regard to either of the two criteria. They make few demands, and their expressions of love or responsiveness to children's needs are limited. None of the younger children of unengaged parents was seen by researchers to be "optimally competent"; when these children were adolescents, they suffered more from anxiety, depression, and substance abuse than any of the others, and they had the lowest academic achievement (Baumrind, 2008).

At the other end of the spectrum are what Baumrind (2008) labeled *authoritative* parents. These are the parents who have high demands and expectations for their children, and who are similarly high in responding to their kids' needs. Authoritative parents are attentive to their children's needs (p. 18); they "encourage individuality and independence; they are warm and understanding of their child's perspective" (p. 20). When authoritative parents do make demands of their children, "they accompany their demands with explanations to help the child understand the parent's conception of appropriate behavior" (p. 21). The children of Baumrind's authoritative parents were found to be both more community-oriented and more self-regulated than their peers.

Baumrind's two other parenting styles are high in one of the variables and low in the other: *permissive* parenting is characterized by good nurturance but very few demands, whereas the parent described as *authoritarian* makes lots of demands, even commands, but with very little responsiveness to the child's needs. The children raised by permissive parents—adults who supplied lots of "love" but did not burden their children by placing demands on them—were seen by researchers as "not self-regulated, prosocial, or achievement-oriented; when they became adolescents, these children were more likely to abuse drugs than were children whose parents were more demanding" (p. 19). The children of authoritarian parents also suffered more from anxiety and depression than their peers; similarly, they had lower academic skills and were found to give in to peer pressure more than others (p. 20).

Though Baumrind's research was carried out very much apart from the research by self-determination theorists, the significant overlap in their findings is difficult to ignore: the healthiest, most community oriented and most self-regulated young people are those who have been treated with a consistent diet of structure/expectations/demands (all these being supported by explanatory rationale, when appropriate) and a nurturant support characterized as "warm, responsive, and autonomy-supportive" (Baumrind, 2008, p. 21). Let us look at two key words in the concept of relatedness: warmth and responsiveness.

Warmth

In his article on "Teachers as Facilitators: What Autonomy Supportive Teachers Do and Why Their Students Benefit," Johnmarshall Reeve (2006) noted that relatedness "occurs when teachers create the conditions in which students feel special and important to the teacher; it revolves around a teacher-provided sense of warmth, affection, and approval for students" (pp. 232-233). In a similar vein, Richard Ryan told participants at one of CSEE's Institutes for Character Development Leaders that perhaps the most powerful indicator of relatedness at school is when a student can say "My teacher likes me." If our aim is for students' demonstrations of character to be internally motivated, Ryan (with colleague Christopher Niemiec), reports that students "tend to internalize and accept as their own the values and practices of those to whom they feel, or want to feel, connected, and from contexts in which they experience a sense of belonging." Niemiec and Ryan follow this statement with the observation that, in the classroom, "relatedness is deeply associated with a student feeling that the teacher genuinely likes, respects, and values him or her" (Niemiec & Ryan, 2009, p. 139).

Despite these descriptors, warmth is hard to put into words, and perhaps equally hard to conjure through an act of the will. Moreover, it is difficult to train people to be warm, other than through their practicing some of the actions just described: behaving respectfully toward students, attempting to value students and their efforts, looking for what might be special in each student, and seeking to show students that they, and their efforts, are approved of.

In an overview article on self-determination theory, Ryan and Deci (2000b) noted the role that relatedness plays, in their assertion that "the primary reason people initially perform [extrinsically motivated] actions is because the behaviors are prompted, modeled, or valued by significant others to whom they feel (or want to feel) attached or related" (p. 73). In the same vein, Ryan and Deci cite previous research, in line with theirs, where students "who felt securely connected to, and cared for by, their parents and teachers" had more fully internalized the regulation for positive behavior in school (p. 73). The message is thus that teachers who can establish relationships of trust and care have students whose good behavior becomes internally motivated, as opposed to externally regulated.

Though some individuals seem to have a natural warmth, most of us feel more of it in some situations and with some people than in others. Surroundings have much to do with one's perception of warmth, especially social surroundings. The importance of working on school climate and culture thus comes immediately to mind (in this regard, see especially Lickona & Davidson, 2005; Elbot & Fulton,

2008). In our interactions with students, we know that eye contact and appropriate physical distance/proximity can influence the sense of warmth, as can a number of other factors regarding the ways we interact. Showing interest in a student's life beyond the classroom, if done genuinely (and unpryingly), also conveys warmth; and certainly anything a teacher can do to increase a student's sense of autonomy or competence is perceived positively. On the whole, though, and as important as this facet of relatedness is, it is difficult to make practical suggestions for increasing the kind of warmth that is generated from within. Lots of what is perceived resides in how something is done, rather than in what is done. In this sense it is a spiritual characteristic.

Responsiveness

Responsiveness is not necessarily easily conjured, either, but there are aspects to responsiveness that allow for conscious attention. The power of responsiveness—at its most basic level, the power of an adult "being there" for a child's needs—was described in the 1950s, 60s, and into the 70s in the writings of John Bowlby and Mary Ainsworth (see Watson & Ecken, 2003, for a summary). As the early proponents and explicators of attachment theory, Bowlby and Ainsworth observed one-year-olds and the conditions under which they developed a secure attachment to their mothers. The primary factor at very early ages was that of proximity, when the child could be certain that his or her mother was near. The sense of safety offered by maternal proximity allowed young children to explore their immediate environment. Parents who consistently responded to their young children's need for "presence" saw them develop secure attachments; those who were rarely available or only intermittently available had children who developed "insecure attachment" relationships.

The need for parental proximity evident in attachment theorists' observations of very young children does not disappear as children grow older, though greater distance and longer stretches of time between assurances of proximity come with maturity.

Baumrind and her colleagues studied children who were older than those studied by Bowlby and Ainsworth, and thus children whose needs expanded commensurately. The same is true for self-determination theory researchers. A wider range of needs is to be expected in older children, but it deserves focus here. The writings of the researchers cited in this chapter, as throughout the book, are rife with references to the words *responsiveness* and *needs*—nearly always in the sense of responsiveness *to* needs, and in our case, *responsiveness to the needs of students*. Some references are limited to the need for autonomy, because of its being the focus of a particular writing. For example, in an article on motivation and education, Ryan and Powelson state: "often one feels most related to those who are responsive to one's autonomous expressions" (1991, p. 53); and we read in Reeve and colleagues (2004) that autonomy-supportive teachers who work to bring "students' self-determined inner motives [into line with] their classroom activity [do so] by identifying and nurturing students' needs" (p. 148). Note that even in this latter case, in an article about autonomy support ("Enhancing Students' Engagement by Increasing Teachers' Autonomy Support"), the authors are speaking to the benefits of educators' responsiveness to a broader set of needs than just the need for autonomy.

Responsiveness to the needs of well-being

Chapter 2 of this book proposed that education's purpose—the ultimate goal that gathers together and gives both meaning and perspective to good citizenship, lifelong learning, successful careers, and other worthwhile aspirations—is to promote the kind of well-being that allows for each of those lifelong-learning citizens to flourish in his or her own individual, meaningful way. Chapter two also proposed that the purpose of character education is to foster in students the skills, and the will, to nurture the well-being of those around them. When we struggle to define the best ways to foster relatedness with students, our struggle points to one reason why being conscious of purpose makes a difference. After all, what connection between human beings could be stronger, healthier, and more durable than a relationship where one person is committed to helping fulfill another's needs for well-being? To recap this in terms of Carol Ryff's set of well-being markers from chapter 2, is there a more beneficent form of relatedness than the one felt by a student who perceives her teacher as attempting to nurture the following?

- self acceptance, such that she feels generally positive about herself, about her skills, her talents, and her life, even while acknowledging and accepting that some of her skills and talents are better and some are weaker than others;

- relationships, meaning her understanding of the give and take of human relationships and her ability to engage in warm, satisfying, and trusting relationships with others; her capacities for empathy, affection and intimacy;

- autonomy, so that she is the one who sets the direction of her life, so that she is learning to be an independent thinker, and is able to resist outside pressures to form opinions or act in certain ways;

- competence, where she feels she has the academic, social, and other skills to meet the challenges that life and most future situations will present;

- a sense of purpose in life, and some of the skills needed to fulfill that purpose; and

- a continued path of growth, being open to new experiences, realizing her personal potential, and growing in ways that reflect greater self-knowledge and increased effectiveness.

Reeve seems to be referring to many of these in description of teachers working on relatedness:

> *Attuned teachers know these things because they listen closely to what their students say and make a special effort to be aware of what their students want and need. . . When they support their students' capacities for self-direction, teachers accept students as they are, provide encouragement, and assist them in their efforts to realize the goals they set for themselves (2006, p. 232-233).*

Practical examples: nurturing relatedness

Unconditional positive regard

Strive to develop and show what psychologist Carl Rogers referred to as unconditional positive regard. A well-known psychotherapist in the mid-20th century, Rogers coined the term to describe the importance of attempting to communicate warmth and acceptance in interactions, regardless of the other's opinions or behavior. This attitude, especially toward students struggling in class, is known to be one of the factors that helps internalize motivation.

Verbal interactions with students

Relatedness in the classroom is illustrated in a study done by Reeve and his colleagues (1999). The researchers studied the verbal interactions that pre-service teachers had with their students, and the effects of these interactions on the students' motivation. After controlling for the students' initial level of motivation, five kinds of utterances by teachers correlated significantly with motivating style. These teachers
- were more likely to ask about the students' wants
- were more likely to respond to student-generated questions
- offered more statements that showed they tried to see things from the students' perspectives
- were less likely to use directives (e.g., you should do it this way; you must do it as directed)
- were less likely to give students the answer (p. 542).

Other strategies or actions
- eye contact
- show interest in students' lives outside the classroom: sports, hobbies, music, reading, pets, and so forth.
- see a number of strategies in chapter 5 of Lickona & Davidson's *Smart and Good High Schools* (available as PDF download at http://www2.cortland.edu/centers/character/resources/SandG/
- Hal Urban's *Lessons from the Classroom: 20 Good Things Teachers Do* is an excellent resource for building positive relationships in the classroom.

10

Competence

Think about being invited somewhere for a long weekend. The plan is for everyone to spend a joyous three days immersed in precisely that activity for which you have the least talent and (perhaps therefore) the least interest. Let's say the weekend is planned such that the last afternoon will be devoted to a contest, with prizes awarded for the best performances. And of course everyone will participate!

Most of us prefer to avoid such situations. That's a piece of what competence, or rather lack of competence, feels like. One difference is that the scenario you imagined probably involves an activity that was not important in your life. When skill-dependent activities happen at school, however, and you are a kid, you can't just decline the invitation like you can for the weekend. You're stuck. People's eyes are on you; not only are they watching, but frequently they are judging. Some might even relish in your klutziness.

In self-determination theory, competence refers to the perception that one has the skills needed to meet the challenges of life. Like autonomy and relatedness, competence is not just a good idea, it is a human need. Psychological, emotional, and social functioning all suffer when a sense of competence is missing. Those of us who feel like we can't dance, can't sing, or can't write computer code can usually manage to stay off the dance floor, or out of those other scenarios where our incompetence would stand out. But if you feel like you can't read, it's pretty hard to stay out of the classroom, unless, of course, misbehavior can get you sent to the principal's office.

Many kids would rather be seen as troublemakers than as dumb, incompetent. Most educators grew up with the social and academic competencies needed to meet school's primary challenges. But think about the student who perceives his or her social skills, or academic skills, to be completely lacking.

Edward Deci, Richard Ryan, and their colleagues who have looked extensively at competence as it applies to education describe it in terms of "having control over outcomes, being self-efficacious, having confidence, and having the strategies and capacities for success" (Deci et al., 1991, p. 339). Competence in the social domain involves different sets of skills. The essence of competence lies in a certain amount of *confidence* that, even though challenges lie ahead, our *skills* give us a fair chance of navigating successfully through those challenges. If we are not confident of being able to accomplish them, competence might also include knowing we can strategize a way to extricate ourselves from a situation without causing others much difficulty, or ourselves much embarrassment.

A sense of competence comes in part from the realization that one has grown and thus will continue to grow. A 9th grader, for example, may not have the skills to do college work, but still be relatively confident that she will have those skills in another three years. Similarly, for a young man frightened about knowing how to talk to his grandfather who was just diagnosed with cancer, a sense of competence may assure him that if he watches others and thinks through things, he will probably be okay.

One perspective on competence in the weekend scenario might concern our knowing how to renegotiate conditions, saying something to the dancers or the computer coders like "how about if you all do your thing, and let me do the cooking?" All three areas of action—participating fully, extricating oneself gracefully, or renegotiating a more comfortable role—take certain skills. The better such skills are mastered, the better we feel about ourselves and the healthier our social interactions are.

For the purposes of this chapter, let's look at three of the key elements touched on above: skills, confidence, and the tangential but important area of challenge.

Skills

The word skills figures prominently in definitions of competence. Skill sets come in a variety of areas, but not all of them fill the need for our perception of competence. I went to elementary school with a boy who could play that famous bit from the William Tell Overture on his front teeth by flipping his fingernails against them. As fun as his musical performance was, the challenges of life in elementary school are broader and deeper. A certain level of academic competence is essential if kids are to survive, and thrive, at school. Because school also involves interaction with others, it is impossible to have a satisfactory school experience without certain social skills, also. Fortunately, in addition to his musical prowess (and good athletic skills), my schoolmate was also both academically and socially adept. These last three areas—academics, social life, and athletics—probably represent the three skill areas that carry the most currency for students today, though social and academic competencies certainly are the two most salient.

Much successful work has been done by university scholars to establish the link between social and emotional competencies and the way they affect both academic success and general well-being in students. Most notable is perhaps the work at the Collaborative for Academic, Social, and Emotional Learning (CASEL), at the University of Illinois at Chicago (http://www.casel.org/about). This research is part of the reason why these competencies are being increasingly recognized as vital components of character initiatives (see, e.g., Weissberg et al., 2013). The beneficial effects of mastering certain social and emotional skills have also contributed to why we are hearing the acronym SEL more often in education today, and why some schools are beginning to use it in lieu of character education.

Confidence

Skills and confidence go hand in hand with the concept of competence. To have skills without confidence suggests an unfair lack of self-appreciation. Confidence without skills, on the other hand, is an unhealthy self-delusion.

Carol Dweck's explanation of the importance and power of a "growth mindset" as opposed to a "fixed mindset" touches on the confidence aspect of competence. The growth mindset may rank as one of the important educational ideas of the early 21st century. In one passage of the book Dweck wrote to introduce the concept to the general public—*Mindset: The New Psychology of Success* (2006)—she offers a poignant vignette from a class where the growth mindset was being taught. The teacher was explaining how people who end up being successful in life tend to reach success much more from hard work and continued effort than from their native abilities. The explanation aimed to help students understand that we might be born with certain intellectual, artistic, athletic and other abilities, but these abilities are not the same as the ways we develop them through practice; our abilities expand and grow through practice. The skills of art, athletics, and the intellect that grow with effort and exercise are what lead to success. Super Bowl rings and best selling novels belong only to those who put in the effort. Dweck recounts that after the growth mindset explanation:

> *All at once Jimmy, the most hard-core turned-off low-effort kid in the group, looked up with tears in his eyes and said "You mean I don't have to be dumb?" From that day on he worked. He started staying up late to do his homework, which he never used to bother with at all. He started handing in assignments early so he could get feedback and revise them (p. 59).*

Let's look at Jimmy in light of the definition of competence used above: one's perception of having the skills to meet, and to have success with, the challenges of life. The skills are necessary, but not quite sufficient. From a self-determination perspective, competence ideally requires that an individual have the skills, and at the same time have the feeling (confidence, perception) that the skills will work. What Jimmy experienced was less about skills, at least for now, than it was about his sense of self-efficacy—that he was capable of taking on the challenge of developing the skills; it illustrates how the two work together. Most of us who are confident about our skills achieve this confidence because we have been able to exercise those skills and have success with them. Jimmy managed to glean enough confidence—at least in academics—from Dweck's explanation that he was willing to exercise his capacities for academic work thereafter, and gain skills, and competence, from his experience.

Some of Dweck's mindset research relates to resilience, in terms of how students cope with failure. Competence is one factor in resilience; when a person believes that "I have the skills to survive this setback," there is more impetus to begin the work needed to emerge from the setback.

The mindset theory posits that the kind of mindset we develop is due in part to the way people interact with us. Parents and teachers thus play pivotal roles. When kids hear what is called *person praise*—phrases suggesting *permanent* traits like "You're so talented," "You're such a good athlete," "You're a natural"—the subtle message is that smartness or talent is inborn; it's not going to change much. The more kids hear such messages, the more likely the messages are to "stick." The role of effort is naturally downplayed in a fixed mindset; after all, they start to believe that success or failure is due primarily to inherent ability. So kids with a fixed mindset tend to put out less effort and try fewer strategies; a "natural" doesn't need to practice that much. Ultimately, what research has shown is that when kids with fixed mindsets hit a roadblock or experience a setback, they tend to respond with a greater sense of helplessness because they have less experience with continuing to tackle a challenge (Kamins & Dweck, 1999).

Teachers should also be aware, at least in the intellectual domain, of some of the negative side effects of a fixed mindset. In a series of three studies that Dweck engaged in with colleagues (Hong et al., 1999), the results indicated that students with fixed mindsets "are likely to engage in behaviors, like withdrawing effort or procrastinating, that will jeopardize their chances for success but will give them face-saving excuses for poor performance" (p. 597). In other words, saving face is more important than struggling to master material.

Christopher Niemiec and Richard Ryan (2009) point to three things teachers can do to foster competence. One is giving students experiences with success. The importance of engineering success experiences for students should be self-evident, as such experiences are natural builders of confidence. The second is fostering students' sense of self-efficacy, which points not just to the confidence of having been through something successfully before, but rather to a certain amount of confidence in facing something new. Self-efficacy is what Jimmy gained from the growth mindset explanation. I remember seeing a friend pick up a woodwind that he had never played before and, within less than a minute, being able to play successful notes from a well-known, although quite simple, tune. His experiences with other instruments gave him the confidence that he could deal with this one, too. Helping students understand the concept of a growth mindset is one way to foster self-efficacy. A growth mindset offers a sense of hope: "even if I don't have all the skills I need right now, at least I know that with the right kind of effort, I should be able to develop the skills"; or similarly, "I don't know anything about this, but I probably could get a feel for it with a little practice."

> *Five things teachers can do to promote competence*
> - *give all students experience with success*
> - *help students remember past success experiences*
> - *foster a sense of self-efficacy in students (mindset)*
> - *offer optimal challenges to the extent possible*
> - *offer positive performance feedback (ch. 11)*

Optimal challenges

The third recommendation Niemiec and Ryan make for teachers wanting to help students fill their need for competence is to present students with activities that are optimally challenging. Though far from many educators' favorite topic, the video game continues to offer a compelling illustration of the power of optimal challenges. Myriad are the educators who have lamented what they perceived as students squandering time on video games. One of the primary reasons for the attraction lies precisely in the way such games are constructed. Each level offers a level of difficulty greater than the one that preceded it. If you try to come into the game at too high a level, you get knocked out, knocked down, or knocked in some other way that is not fun. On the other hand, if you are an experienced player, there is not much fun going back to the lowest levels, either. It's all engineered to help the player find that level of challenge that best meets his or her current skills, and to keep pushing from there. That's optimal: not too hard, not too easy, just right there where all your attention is needed, building confidence that, with a combination of attention and effort, that level, too, can be mastered.

Human beings need to grow. We need to stretch ourselves. Watch a toddler (assuming that the toddler is securely attached, as discussed in the last chapter), where everything is about curiosity, exploration. We need new challenges. We learn best when the challenge is appropriate. More importantly, we do not feel competent, in any area, until we have met a challenge we were faced with, and succeeded in it. In other words, the competence does not really develop until the behavior is "effectively enacted": the challenge has to be met successfully.

This is one area where teachers, parents, and tutors end up undermining the growth of children. Reeve and colleagues' research, referred to in the "practical examples" for relatedness at the end of the last chapter, noted that when teachers "were less likely to give students the answer," they ended up being more likely to help students internalize motivation. The reason why is that the teacher who gives away the answer too quickly is interfering with the student's development of competence: the student has less opportunity to grapple, and to come up with it him- or herself. Similarly, when parents or tutors help students with their assigments, that "help" is building competence only if the student feels that he is responsible for the work completed. If a student feels like his completed assignment, or the A on his paper, was due to his tutor's efforts or his parents' revisions, no competence is fostered. The success must be perceived as autonomous.

The reason optimal challenges play such an important role in one's sense of competence is that they ramp up the power of a successful experience, and thus they do a better job of giving people the sense that skills are developing. Richard Ryan and Cynthia Powelson speak specifically to this, as it relates to education, in their description of competence as concerning "the sense of accomplishment and effectance that derives from the exercise of one's capacities under conditions of optimal challenge" (1991, p. 52). Think about the first time you successfully played a very difficult piece of music, or did something athletically, or performed well in some other field that required lots of practice and a certain level of skill. The element of satisfaction—the sense of confidence, the sense of competence—is much greater than doing something simpler. The more difficult the challenge, the greater the sense of competence is fostered.

The other side of this coin is when challenges are beyond optimal. Those of us with numerous success experiences in our past can put up with lots of failure. But when we start to realize that we don't have the skill for something, because we are failing in it too often, then it becomes either boring or painful to continue. This range between success that is too easy and lack of success because it is too hard is what we need to find with students. The benefits in the optimal range are as much social and psychological as they are academic. Kids who feel like they are continual academic failures will drop out, psychologically if not physically. But dropping out does not mean the human need for competence is filled; it needs to be filled in some way, so students will seek ways if educators or parents cannot fill the need: sports, drama, teasing and taunting, getting the teacher's goat, making explosives...or whatever. The possibilities are endless.

The challenge for the educator, then, is to attempt to look at every class (and ideally at every student) with an eye toward answering the question "What is the most important challenge to face these students with in order to catalyze their growth toward our school's goals, and what is the optimal level of that challenge?" The challenge needed might be academic, it might be social, it might be emotional; it might arise in some other area. And in light of the previous two chapters, when the challenge is presented it should be seen as inviting (rather than controlling) and as coming from someone who is warmly supportive of student growth.

Let us close this chapter with an opening to the one that follows. It is impossible to be an educator without giving students feedback on what they are doing. The way feedback is given contains tremendous potential for fostering competence, for undermining competence, or for doing neither. Given those choices, and given how beneficial an increased sense of competence is, and especially given the realization that it takes the same amount of time and energy for an adult to offer competence-building feedback as it does to give any other kind of feedback, the desire to foster competence should be a no-brainer. Such feedback can help students be more fully aware of their past successes, or it can help foster self-efficacy, or it can even make suggestions that might make the next challenge more optimal. The next chapter addresses some of the specifics of feedback.

11

Praise, Criticism, and Feedback

In a recent journal article on praise, Eddie Brummelman and his colleagues in the Netherlands reported on their two-part study looking at the ways parents praised children and the effects their praise had (Brummelman et al., 2014). In part one, the researchers focused especially on whether children with low self-esteem were praised differently than those with high self-esteem. They were. As a matter of fact, the team discovered that "parents gave children with low self-esteem *more than twice as much person praise* as they did children with high self-esteem" (p. 10, italics mine). Children with high self-esteem, on the other hand, received more *process* praise than children with low self-esteem. Thus, while the high self-esteem children more often got validated for effort or strategy (process praise), their low esteem counterparts heard comments that were more global, comments that attempted to define them as permanently talented or skilled (person praise).

The second study looked at the effects of praise. The researchers concluded that parental efforts to overcome their kids' emotional vulnerability via person praise were perhaps causing the very same vulnerability that the parents were trying to overcome. In this study, children with low self-esteem who experienced person praise ended up feeling shame when they later encountered failure, which was not the case for children praised for strategies or effort. In the researchers' words, "person praise backfires, especially in children with low self-esteem" (p. 12). The children praised for effort or for their strategies did not feel shame, since their success was less tagged to who they were than to what they did. Their failure was situational rather than personal.

Given the location of these findings, in Holland, the critically thinking reader might doubt that the same parenting practices are prevalent in North America; or even wonder, since this is only one set of data, if the results would come out differently in a second or third data set. The skepticism is important, and yet the results of Brummelman and colleagues' second study are not in any way inconsistent with what was already known about person praise and process praise in North America (e.g., Dweck, 2006; Kamins & Dweck, 1999; Dweck et al., 2012). It is this second study's results that I would like to use as a launchpad for a deeper look at praise, criticism, and feedback in light of the chapters that preceded this one.

In the earliest chapters of the Structure section, and again in the last chapter, on competence, we looked at goals. Ideally, our goals for character development should overlap with our goals for education in general. Should the purpose of our praise not, therefore, similarly aim toward accomplishing educational goals when they can? This question is more important than it might initially sound; here's why. Loving teachers and parents—adults responsive to kids' needs—want a lot for the kids under their care. They want kids to feel good, as we assume from the parents Brummelman studied. It's natural. If feeling good were the only goal, then both person praise and process praise would do the job. But most adults have deeper and longer term goals for children. They want feeling good to last; they also want personal growth, responsibility, self-esteem, a sense of self-regulation, the skills of entering into and maintaining friendships, and a number of other things even beyond Carol Ryff's markers of psychological well-being outlined previously. And here's where process praise takes a different route from person praise. The effects of person praise seem to stop with good feelings and short-term motivation; and as Brummelman's study suggested, praising children for "inherent" traits can backfire. Process praise, on the other hand, manages to achieve all of what the person praise wanted and a whole lot more, but without the backfire effect.

Let's do a short examination of a number of types of feedback, with attention to the effects each type seems to have in regard to the last three chapters. We will refer to the chart on page 110, where the columns along the right side of the chart indicate whether the type of feedback either fosters (upward arrow), or does not foster (downward arrow), autonomy (A), relatedness (R), competence (C), or motivation (M).

Process praise supports autonomy and competence

The most common explanation for why praising a student's effort or strategy is healthier than praising talents or abilities is that it engenders a growth mindset. That's one factor in competence. When the student realizes that growth is attainable through effort or strategy, he or she is more disposed to keep trying; the idea of inborn abilities is no longer a limiting factor. Let's look at this praise phenomenon from a self-determination perspective, which goes a little deeper than just growth mindset.

Statements like "You solved that problem because you're so smart" or "Well of course you won! You're a natural athlete!" heavily discount any autonomy on the part of the student. They imply that inborn smarts or athletic skill were responsible for the victory, rather than the student's (autonomous) efforts. Process praise on the other hand, with its focus on effort or strategy, suggests that the student was in control of what was accomplished: "Of course you won! Every time you got blocked, you looked for a new way to get around the obstacle!" Process praise thus tends to validate, and to encourage, autonomous development. It helps nurture self-regulation and it helps internalize motivation: two reasons why process praise is preferable.

Person praise similarly does nothing to foster competence. Because its focus is on inborn—and basically unchangeable—traits, it offers no suggestion that a young person can do something to increase his or her chances for success in meeting life's challenges. Process praise, on the other hand, validates extra effort or new strategy. It suggests that being flexible and perseverant can help the student increase skills—what competence is all about—thus opening the road to further successes.

Note that both process praise and person praise are positive, and thus they may be equally efficacious in fostering or maintaining relatedness. Though both can lead to an increase in motivation, motivation might be expected to last longer when it is bolstered by autonomy, relatedness, and competence rather than only relatedness.

feedback type	characteristics	A	R	C	M
positive performance feedback	observations on specific positive aspects of an action; PPF may include suggestions to enhance or improve performance next time	→	→	→	→
process praise	positive judgment regarding effort or strategy that made performance successful	→	→	→	→
simple positive feedback	positive judgment about performance, but lacking information that clarifies what was positive		→	→	→
directives	commands or suggestions that are perceived by students as attempts to control or steer activity in the direction of the adult's wishes	←	←		←
negative information	information or observations regarding why an activity was unsuccessful		←	→	
person praise	positive remarks that suggest an action was successful because of inborn or otherwise permanent characteristics of the student		→		→
negative feedback	negative opinions expressed regarding performance, with no information to clarify why performance was unsatisfactory	←	←	←	←
hurtful words	utterances expressing negative opinions of the student, for the purpose of psychological control or manipulating behavior	←	←	←	←

Arrows indicate the tendency for feedback to increase or decrease filling students' needs for autonomy (A), relatedness (R), competence (C), or motivation (M)

Only process praise thus offers the chance for meeting all three needs.

Positive performance feedback may support competence better than person praise

I saw that Madeleine was trying to get you into an argument, and you did a great job not letting her draw you in. The best was how you managed to get her to talk about photography; she completely forgot about the argument!

What you guys did to find a new design after your old model didn't work was brilliant! Whose idea was it to think about reaching out to outside experts?

When we look at praise and feedback from a self-determination theory perspective, it is possible that positive performance feedback does even more than process praise to promote positive development. Both types of feedback look favorably at a student's performance, and they both tend to validate autonomy in the sense that they give the student credit for being the agent, or author, of the act performed. Positive performance feedback allows for a greater degree of specificity, however, in that process praise is often associated exclusively with effort or strategy (e.g., Kamins & Dweck, 1999, p. 835; Dweck et al., 2012, p. 9). In contrast, positive performance feedback focuses on any of a number of other observations the adult might have, thus allowing for a wider array of specific suggestions.

Simple positive feedback
Great game last night!
It's always good to have your comments in class discussions.
This was a stellar composition.
You did a super job leading that meeting today.

Simple positive feedback tends to express both personal warmth and approval for an act accomplished. Such feedback does promote further motivation, though its effects appear to be limited. As the examples above suggest, simple positive feedback does little to foster autonomy, and similarly little to foster competence. All in all, such feedback has a positive valence, and therefore can be beneficial, but if an additional half sentence of information can turn positive feedback into positive performance feedback or process praise—and thus do so much more good—why stop at simple feedback?

Feedback to be avoided

Now let's look at the types of feedback that sink toward the bottom of the chart, all of which fall into the category of feedback types to be eschewed by anyone whose goals for children include internalized motivation or psychosocial well-being. Some readers might recall a personal experience where each of these feedback types has led to a positive outcome. Granted this possibility, the utterances on the lower part of the chart ended up toward the bottom because, despite an occasional success, their track records are dismal due to the way they undermine, and in some cases even damage, the good work we want to do. Each of these procedures impedes fulfillment of one or more of the human needs discussed earlier: they attempt to control or manipulate (the opposite of autonomy), they erode the warmth in relationships, or they undermine competence either by eroding confidence or by their failure to offer new avenues for skill development. A diminished ability to explore new avenues for action was what allowed helplessness to set in, in our earlier discussion of person praise and how it undermines resilience.

Directives

All your compositions must be broken into three parts.
Apologize before you go out to recess.
Write an essay about how Leaman was a better president than Sandlin.
You should ask me before using those materials.
You'll need to do the easy problems before you try the ones in section B.

Directives represent the very antithesis of autonomy support, which is the main reason they are to be discouraged. A directive is a teacher's attempt to bend students to his or her way of thinking or preferred way of acting. Part of what students perceive as controlling comes from tone of voice, the sometimes almost nonverbal way some teachers have of saying "You're going to do this my way, or else." Much of the rest lies in verbal content, which often includes words like "should" and "must."

Directives can undermine relationships, especially via the bossy teacher voice. If they have a positive side, it is that they do occasionally offer hints that might lead to competence, as when a teacher's directive is indeed the most effective way to attack a problem. The major problem with directives however is that "people experience them as controllers of their behavior" (Ryan & Deci, 2000a, p. 59); the autonomy they remove is a key element in motivation and self-regulation. So even if the teacher's directive happens to be the brilliant "only way," it tends to block students' interest in searching for other ways in future trials. A far more effective strategy is for the teacher to offer the utterance in the form of a suggestion, as an option for students to consider, and then to accompany it with an explanatory rationale. Remember, we are addressing character development as long-term growth in self-managed behaviors and concern for others rather than short term compliance with adults' wishes. When students perceive that the teacher's suggestions tend to be helpful hints that are usually worthwhile, they tend to think about the suggestions, and then adopt them as their own.

This might be a good time to recall a concept embedded in self-determination theory: perception. It is possible to give a suggestion that someone perceives as a command; and it is possible to give a command that is perceived as a suggestion. The way something is said may have more to do with its perception than specifically what is said. The fewer the number of directives *perceived*, the greater the chances for growth.

Another issue regarding perception applies to all forms of feedback discussed here, whether positive or negative. As noted in Deci, Vallerand, Pelletier, and Ryan's (1991) summary of motivational practices that apply to educators, even the positive forms of feedback presented here can end up producing negative results, if students perceive them as "presented in a controlling manner" (p. 336). The authors also make the point that some teacher techniques usually considered "controlling" (and thus underminers of autonomy) can actually be used without doing harm, provided students not perceive the teacher as trying to control them—that is, provided the techniques do not leave students "feeling like pawns" (p 337).

Negative informational feedback
Mrs. Henderson is still upset with you boys for making the second graders get off the baseball diamond yesterday.
I think Emilie was hurt more than she showed when you hit her with your jacket yesterday.

Negative informational feedback category is perhaps superfluous after the discussion of positive performance feedback, because it really is positive performance feedback's counterpart. What negative informational feedback has in its favor is that at least it offers information, and sometimes negative information is helpful. Sometimes it is even needed. CSEE's resident expert on academic integrity, John Roberts, has been a frequent reader of things I have written. After proof reading the script for *Breaking into the Heart of Character*, he informed me that I used the word "entail" to an extent that might irritate some readers. In early chapters for this book, his negative information concerned my (over)use of the phrase "such that." It really would have been condescendingly obvious, if not downright irritating, had John attempted to turn his comments into positive performance feedback with a statement like "David, I really liked the way you used *concerned* instead of that other verb on page 27."

Sometimes negative information can be the quickest way to make a point, and the point can be relatively simple. Despite that, negative feedback of all kinds "has generally been found to decrease intrinsic motivation by decreasing perceived competence, and some studies indicate that lowered perceived competence can leave people feeling amotivated and helpless" (Deci et al., 1991, p. 334). If negative information needs to be forthcoming, tone down the negativity to the extent possible, phrase the negative information in such a way that both the words chosen and the tone of voice are perceived as information rather than judgment or control, and then, when possible, follow any negative information with a positive suggestion. The last of these suggestions is especially valid for students, and even more so when the students in question are not necessarily strong in, or secure about, the skills being addressed. It is the positive suggestion that promotes competence, which negative information is far less effective at doing. Using the sentences from the previous page as examples, this might sound like:

I think Emilie was hurt more than she showed when you hit her with your jacket yesterday. Do you think just asking her to move might have been a better way to get to your hat? Or maybe explaining why you were in a hurry?

Mrs. Henderson is still upset with you boys for making the second graders get off the baseball diamond yesterday. Can you think of a kinder way to deal with that situation?... What about if you had asked an adult to help you figure things out?

John Roberts has always been careful to comment on the positive aspects of my writing, too. If I had ever perceived that his comments were consistently negative, I probably would have gravitated (consciously or unconsciously) toward a different reader. Students do not usually have a choice about who is going to be observing their behavior in the cafeteria or reading their work in the classroom.

Negative feedback
My second grade brother could have written a better letter than this.
That was the worst example of sportsmanship I've seen in years.
Is that apology supposed to get you forgiven?
I could give you a D on this paper, but first I'd need to read it again to see if I could find something worth a D.

Many of the comments that apply to negative informational feedback apply here, too. Simple negative feedback—that is, unfavorable judgment without the information offered in negative informational feedback—does nothing to foster autonomy and tends to corrode relatedness. Moreover, it offers no avenue toward competence. Worse than offering no avenue, it often undermines a student's sense of competence. When so many other options are available, and when positive growth is the goal, why resort to the negative?

Hurtful words are worst of all

Hurtful words are rare in, but unfortunately not absent from, schools. And they are still too common in life. The term refers to words that intend to demean or belittle a child, or to attempt to control or get power over a child through psychologically manipulative language. Shaming or poking fun at a weakness both fit into this category. These utterances include barbs like "Maybe that's why nobody likes you," or "If you weren't so stupid maybe things like that wouldn't happen." Parenting expert Diana Baumrind points to research evidence that what she calls "wounding words" are "an even more potent contributor to children's maladjustment than harsh physical punishment" (2008, p. 22).

Rewards: why contingent rewards are bad

A contingent reward is a reward that depends on some activity or level of performance. It says "If you do this, I'll give you that." Though educators trained in the 1980s and 1990's—perhaps even in the first decade of this century—sometimes learned how to shape behavior through precise administration of rewards and "consequences," what the practice suffered from was its looking at short term goals rather than long term goals.

There is a huge body of literature to show that student behavior can be shaped by offering contingent rewards. If the goal is shaping behavior—bending behavior in the direction we want, or trying to control the behavior—then contingent rewards can be effective. If however the goal is not controlling student behavior—but rather students owning their behavior, students internalizing the motivation for behavior, students managing their own behavior—then the contingent rewards are toxic. The death knell on shaping character through rewards rang definitively around the time the century was closing. In the last twenty-five years of research on education and child rearing, few things have emerged more resoundingly than the damage done by contingent rewards. For a discussion of the topic and the "final" debate about it, especially as it pertains to education, see Deci et al., 2001.

In regard to rewards, there are thus three things to notice. The first is that in attempting to control behavior—even to influence the direction behavior will take—autonomy is being taken away from the student. The second is that the reward diminishes the value of the activity (or academic subject) in question. In other words, if engaging in an activity or learning certain material were valuable, we should not need to offer rewards. Yes, some teachers will counter "But they don't know how valuable it is until they do it!" That is what an explanatory rationale (chapter 8) is for: it helps students understand the value, and thus increases their willingness (autonomy) to engage. The third is that contingent rewards have a proven track record for undermining intrinsic motivation (see Deci et al., 1991, 2001)—and probably for moving extrinsic motivation from the inner rings of the illustration on page 74 to the less productive rings. So the teacher who decides to use such rewards should be aware of the possibilities: short term behavior versus long term goals.

12

On Purpose

> *Purpose is a stable and generalized intention to accomplish something that is at once meaningful to the self and of consequence to the world beyond the self.*
> William Damon

Purpose is not one of self-determination theory's factors, and it is not a human need, at least in the same sense as autonomy, relatedness, and the perception of competence. Purpose is nevertheless a strong motivating factor and an important component of well-being, and because of the positive direction it implies, it is a significant component of mature character development. For those reasons I would like to close this book by encouraging educators at least to plant the seeds of purpose in older students. The four brief points I'd like to make are 1) that too few kids are even thinking about purpose in their lives, 2) that there are numerous benefits to discerning one's purpose in life, 3) that educators can be of valuable service in this regard, and 4) that planting the seeds of purpose takes very little time and no expertise. So why not, especially when the benefits accrue to both character development and academic growth?

Too few kids are thinking about purpose

In his book *The Path to Purpose*, William Damon relates research regarding young people and purpose in life. The work, which he carried out with Kendall Cotton Bronk, Jenni Menon Mariano, and others at Stanford University, indicated that about 20% of young people in their late teens have developed a sense of purpose in life. Another 25% are far from finding purpose, or doing anything serious in regard to it. The remaining 55% of the team's sample was split between a group he referred to as *dreamers*, meaning those who had given some thought to performing noble actions but had no plans for really acting on their ideas; and another group referred to as *dabblers*, who engaged in activities that seemed purposeful, "but who showed little awareness of the meaning of these activities beyond the present," and, consequently, showed "few signs of committing themselves to these pursuits over time" (2008, pp. 59-60).

On a smaller scale, and in a much less scientific manner, I have engaged large groups of high school students a half-dozen times in a series of three questions. The first question was "How many of you have been asked what you want to be when you grow up?" As would be expected with students of any age, nearly all hands raised; I suspect that those who did not raise their hands kept them down more for lack of enthusiasm for a visitor's lame question than for lack of experience with questions about career plans. The second question was "How many of you have ever been asked where you want to go to college?" Given that all these schools have been private independent schools where higher education was on the horizon for at least 95% of the students, I have always expected that nearly everyone would raise a hand. And they have.

The third question put to the students was "How many of you have ever been asked about the purpose of your life?" The number of students raising hands after this question has always been between 20% and (never more than) 30%.

Though Damon's numbers and mine come from very different places, they are not terribly out of sync with one another. The field of research into purpose is still young, but given what we know already about the benefits of having a sense of purpose, it is disheartening, and surprising, that more schools have not engaged students with the issue.

Benefit

Does it matter if schools support the search for purpose? It does, for at least two reasons. The first concerns the number of benefits that seem to accrue to, or at least are associated with, someone who has discerned a purpose for his or her life. Damon's associate Kendall Cotton Bronk, with colleagues Holmes Finch, and Tasneem Talib (2010) reports purpose in life as associated with motivation, psychological health, happiness, life satisfaction, and resiliency (p. 133). Elsewhere, she relates studies where "purpose and substance abuse are inversely related," and where purpose is negatively related to nicotine and food addictions (Bronk, 2014, p. 53). Of course many of the issues just mentioned are complex problems that require complex solutions, and in no way am I suggesting that working on purpose will singlehandedly solve them. Moreover, it is important for readers to be aware that the research on purpose has less history, and thus less depth, than what we have on the power of autonomy, relatedness, and competence. And yet when we look at the little time it takes to invite students in late middle school or high school to consider the value of thinking about purpose in life—together with the possible benefits—there is little to lose and much to gain. Working on purpose will not solve complex problems, but if tobacco use or self-medication in any of a variety of ways is, in some cases, influenced by a lack of meaning in life, then in those cases a sense of purpose is one step in the direction of a solution. Search Institute's Peter Benson (2006) has demonstrated quite convincingly that the more "developmental assets" (of which purpose in life is one) a young person experiences, the lower are his or her chances of having problems with alcohol, tobacco, drugs, depression, violence, and a number of other issues (pp. 80-85).

A second reason why purpose matters relates to its being a factor in well-being. Veronika Huta and Alan Waterman recently illustrated the growing realization of the importance of eudaimonic well-being—the kind of well-being discussed in earlier chapters of this book. They observed that "over twice as many publications have employed eudaimonic terminology since 2008, as did before 2008" (Huta & Waterman, 2014, p. 1426). The Huta & Waterman report focused especially on recent studies of well-being. In the lists of factors composed by the eleven scholars most active in research and publication today, "meaning/purpose" and their synonyms was second only to "growth, realization, self-actualization" as a definitional category for well-being.

Educators can facilitate the process

Damon defined purpose in life as "a stable and generalized intention to accomplish something that is at the same time meaningful to the self and consequential for the world beyond the self" (2008, p. 33; Damon et al., 2003). In his definition, we see echoes not just of the school administrators in chapter two of this book, but of every group that took the survey; every time educators were asked what they hoped their students to be doing 20 years after graduation—the most common answer concerned helping others, doing something to make the world a better place, solving the world's problems, or some endeavor along those lines. Sixty-two percent of the school administrators expressed their greatest hope that their alums would, in accord with Damon's definition of purpose, be "accomplishing something consequential for the world beyond the self."

What is the best age to begin the process? Little research has been done regarding the development of purpose in younger children, probably for developmental reasons. While implying that elementary grades are too young to approach purpose head on, Kendall Cotton Bronk nevertheless asserts in her book *Purpose in Life: A Critical Component of Optimal Youth Development* (2014) that "experiences in childhood can set the stage for later development of purpose." Bronk is one of the leading researchers on youth purpose today, and points to research suggesting that the more positive experiences children have, the "more likely [they are] to report purposes later in life, especially in emerging adulthood" (pp. 69-70). I would submit, parenthetically, that one way to provide some of these positive experiences is to offer students supportive, trusting relationships, and a growing sense both of autonomy and of academic and social-emotional competence.

As children grow into adolescence, things change; adolescents certainly are capable of exploring purpose in life, even if exploration does not always guarantee success. Educators can facilitate the process. According to Sonia Isaac Koshy and Jenni Menon Mariano, "research to date reports a positive relationship between purpose and school and teacher support" (2012, p. 15). But how many schools are engaging students in the search for purpose? My hand raising survey was far from a large or representative sample, but its paltry results suggest that very few schools are even inviting students to consider the question. Nevertheless, asking the question—planting the seeds of thought about life purpose—takes no more time out of a personal conversation, or

Structure & Guts of Character Education

out of a class discussion, than a discussion about college prospects or what the student might want to do with his or her life after graduation. It is not another "prep" for a teacher, and it is not something else on a teacher's plate. It is, rather, a valuable tool for a student's future and an invitation to reflect on a topic of immense intrinsic value.

I would do it this way, in either a formal or an informal setting:

You know, people tend to be much happier when they feel like they have a purpose for their lives. One of the things we know about happiness is that there is more than one kind. Most of us think about the kind that comes from buying things or being the center of attention. That is the kind we hear about most, because we hear about it from advertisers who want to make us "happy" if we buy their products. This kind of happiness feels great, but as you have probably noticed, it does not last long. There is another kind of happiness that is not as flashy, but it is longer lasting and more meaningful. This is the kind of happiness that we feel when we have great relationships with others, when we get to spend time doing things that are meaningful to us, when we feel like we've accomplished something important, and when we have a sense of what the purpose of our lives is.

Most students are able to get a sense of purpose in their lives by the time they graduate from high school. It doesn't always happen by that time, but frequently it does. Some of you might have a sense of purpose already, but if you don't, I would encourage you to give it some thought.

A purpose is something you want to accomplish or a problem you feel like you need to solve. But it's not just anything you want to accomplish, or any problem to solve. A purpose is a long-term goal. It is something that is personally meaningful to you; it might even feel like it's meaningful to you alone, because a purpose in life has to come from inside you, it can't be given to you by someone else. But at the same time that a purpose in life is meaningful to you, it also involves other people, because the kind of purpose that gives people the most satisfaction with their lives is the kind where the problem you want to solve, or the thing you want to accomplish, is something to help other people, or to make the world or your community a better place.

Once you have your sense of purpose, it doesn't mean you're stuck with it. Frequently, as people grow, their sense of purpose grows too; it might change as you become aware of new things or have new experiences. But you feel much better, and you feel like whatever you are doing has more quality when it is working toward your purpose.

As stated earlier, any teacher who works with adolescents in the classroom has the skills to offer guidance of the type just suggested. It takes no special expertise and requires no real time commitment. A whole course on purpose would be overkill. Even a whole unit is probably too much. But it should be revisited or reinforced from time to time in a non-pressured and encouraging manner. If no one ever dangles in front of young people the wisdom of purpose in life—as well as the possibility of happiness that is deeper and longer lasting than what consumerism engenders—how are we to expect numbers greater than what Damon's research found or my hand raising produced?

As closing words, note this, too. The only purpose in life that is meaningful is the purpose that is autonomously discerned. We cannot assign purpose to students, any more than we can allow someone else to tell us what is most meaningful in our lives.

"But what if students pick a bad purpose?" Young people involved in relationships of warmth and trust, who feel like they have been taught the skills to face the challenges of life, and who feel like they are acting (autonomously) in ways that they value, in ways that they have chosen, will not pick a bad purpose.

References

Assor, A., Kaplan, H., & Roth, G. (2002). Choice is good, but relevance is excellent: Autonomy-enhancing and suppressing teacher behaviors predicting students' engagement in schoolwork. *British Journal of Educational Psychology*, 72, 261-278.

Baumrind, D. (2013). Authoritative parenting revisited: History and current status. In R.E. Larzelere, A. Sheffield Morris, & A.W. Harris (Eds.), *Authoritative parenting: Synthesizing nurturance and discipline for optimal child development*. Washington, D.C.: American Psychological Association.

Baumrind, D. (2008). Authoritative parenting for character and competence. In D. Streight, *Parenting for Character: Five Experts, Five Practices*. Portland, OR: CSEE Publications.

Baumrind, D. (1991a). The influence of parenting style on adolescent competence and substance abuse. *Journal of Early Adolescence*, 11, 56-95.

Baumrind, D. (1991b). Parenting styles and adolescent development. In R. Lerner, A.C. Petersen, & J. Brooks-Gunn (Eds.), *The encyclopedia on adolescence* (pp. 758-772). New York: Garland.

Berkowitz, M. W. (2012). *You can't teach through a rat, and other epiphanies for educators*. Boone, North Carolina: Character Development Group, Inc.

Berkowitz, M. W. (n.d.). A primer for evaluating a character education initiative. Washington, D.C.: The Character Education Partnership.

Berkowitz, M.W. & Bier, M. (2005). What works in character education? A resource-based guide for practitioners. Washington, D.C.: Character Education Partnership.

References

Bok, D. (2010). *The Politics of Happiness: What government can learn from the new research on well-being*. Princeton, New Jersey: Princeton University Press.

Bronk, K.C. (2014). *Purpose in life: A critical component of optimal youth development*. New York: Springer.

Bronk, K.C., Finch, W.H., & Talib, T.L. (2010). Purpose in life among high ability adolescents. *High Ability Studies*, 21, 133-154.

Brummelman, E., Thomaes, S., Overbeek, G., Orobio de Castro, B., van den Hout, M.A., & Bushman, B.J. (2014). On feeding those hungry for praise: Person praise backfires in children with low self-esteem. *Journal of Experimental Psychology*. 143, 9-14.

Buff, A., Reusser, K., Rakoczy, K. & Pauli, C. (2011). Activating Positive Affective Experiences in the Classroom: "Nice to Have" or Something More? *Learning and Instruction*, 21, 452-466.

Bureau, J.S & Mageau, G.A. (2014). Parental autonomy support and honesty: The mediating role of identification with the honesty value and perceived costs and benefits of honesty. *Journal of Adolescence*, 37, 225-236.

Clark, A. & Senik, C. (2011). Is happiness different from flourishing? Cross-country evidence from the ESS. Working Paper #2011-04. Paris-Jourdan Sciences Economiques.

Damon, W. (2008). *The path to purpose: Helping our youth find their calling in life*. New York, NY: Free Press.

Damon, W., Menon, J., & Bronk, K.C. (2003). The development of purpose during adolescents. *Applied Developmental Science*, 7, 119-128.

Deci, E.L., Vallerand, R.J., Pelletier, L.G., & Ryan, R.M. (1991). Motivation and education: The self-determination perspective. *Educational Psychologist*, 26, 325-346.

Deci, E.L., Eghrari, H., Patrick, B.C., & Leone, D.R. (1994). Facilitating internalization: The self-determination theory perspective. *Journal of Personality*, 62, 119-142.

Deci, E.L., Koestner, R., & Ryan, R.M. (2001). Extrinsic rewards and intrinsic motivation in education: Reconsidered once again. *Review of Educational Research*, 71, 1-27.

DeRoche, E.F. (2004). *Evaluating Character Development: 51 tools for measuring success*. Chapel Hil, N.C.: Character Development Group.

Diener, E., Oishi, S., & Lucas, R.E. (2015). National accounts of subjective well-being. *American Psychologist*, 70, 234-232.

Dweck, C.S. (2006). *Mindset: The new psychology of success*. New York, NY: Random House.

Dweck, C.S., Walton, G.M. & Cohen, G.L. (2012) Academic tenacity: Mindsets and skills that promote long term learning. Paper prepared for the Gates Foundation.

Elbot, C.F. & Fulton D. (2008) *Building an intentional school culture: Excellence in academics and character*. Thousand Oaks, California: Corwin Press.

Farkas, M.S. & Grolnick, W.S. (2010). Examining the components and concomitants of parental structure in the academic domain. *Motivation and Emotion*, 34, 266-279.

Gagné, M. (2003). The role of autonomy support and autonomy orientation in prosocial behavior engagement. *Motivation and Emotion*, 27, 199-223.

Gill, S. and Thomson, G. (2012) *Rethinking Secondary Education: A human centred approach*. Essex, England: Pearson Education Limited.

Grolnick, W.S. & Ryan, R.M. (1987). Autonomy in children's learning: An experimental and individual differences investigation. *Journal of Personality and Social Psychology*, 52, 890-898.

References

Hong, Y., Chiu, C., Dweck, C.S., Derrick, M.-S., & Wan, W. (1999). Implicit theories, attributions, and coping: A meaning system approach. *Journal of Personality and Social Psychology*, 77, 588-599.

Huppert, F.A. & So, T.T.C. (2009). What percentage of people in Europe are flourishing and what characterises them? Florence: Paper prepared for the OECD/ISQOLS meeting "Measuring subjective well-being: an opportunity for NSO's?"

Huta, V. & Waterman, A.S. (2014). Eudaimonia and its distinction from hedonia: Developing a classification and terminology for understanding conceptual and operational definitions. *Journal of Happiness Studies*, 15, 1425-1456. DOI 10.1007/s10902-013-9485-0.

Iyengar, S.S. & Lepper, M.R. (2000). When choice is demotivating: Can one desire too much of a good thing? *Journal of Personality and Social Psychology*, 79, 995-1006

Jang, H., Reeve, J., & Deci, E.L. (2010). Engaging students in learning activities: It is not autonomy support or structure but autonomy support and structure. *Journal of Educational Psychology*, 102, 588-600.

Jordan, A.E. (2001) College student cheating: The role of motivation, perceived norms, attitudes, and knowledge of institutional policy. *Ethics & Behavior*, 11, 233-247.

Josephson Institute of Ethics (2012). 2012 Report Card on the Ethics of American Youth. http://charactercounts.org/programs/reportcard/

Kage, M. & Namiki, H. (1990). The effects of evaluation structure on children's intrinsic motivation and learning. *Japanese Journal of Educational Psychology*, 38, 36-45.

Kamins, M.L. & Dweck, C.S. (1999). Person versus process praise and criticism: Implications for contingent self-worth and coping. *Developmental Psychology*, 35, 833-847.

Koestner, R., Ryan, R.M., Bernieri, F., & Holt, K. (1984). Setting limits on children's behavior: the differential effects of controlling vs informational styles on intrinsic motivation and creativity. *Journal of Personality*, 52, 233-248.

Koshy, S.I. & Mariano, J.M. (2012). Promoting youth purpose: A review of the literature. In J.M. Mariano (Ed.) *New Directions for Youth Development: Support and Instruction for Youth Purpose*. San Francisco, CA: Jossey-Bass.

La Guardia, J.G., Ryan, R.M., Couchman, C.E., & Deci, E.L. (2000). Within-person variation in security of attachment: A self-determination theory perspective on attachment, need fulfillment, and well-being. *Journal of Personality and Social Psychology*, 79, 367-384.

Lickona, T. & Davidson, M. (2005). *Smart & good high schools: Integrating and ethics for success in school, work, and beyond*. Cortland, NY: Center for the 4th and 5th Rs (Respect & Responsibility)/ Washington, D.C.: Character Education Partnership.

McCabe, D. & Treviño, L. K. (1993). Academic dishonesty: Honor codes and other contextual influences. *Journal of Higher Education*, 64, 5, 522-538.

Niemiec, C. & Ryan, R.M. (2009). Autonomy, competence, and relatedness in the classroom: Applying self-determination theory to educational practice. *Theory and Research in Education*, 7, 2, 133-144.

Noddings, N. (2003) *Happiness in education*. New York: Cambridge University Press.

Nucci, L.P. (2009). *Nice is not enough: Facilitating moral development*. Upper Saddle River, NJ: Pearson Education, Inc.

Randall, C. & Corp, A.(2014). Measuring national well-being: European comparisons, 2014. Office for National Statistics. http://www.ons.gov.uk/ons/dcp171766_363811.pdf

Reeve, J., Jang, H., Hardre, P., & Omura, M. (2002). Providing a rationale in an autonomy-supportive way as a strategy to motivate others during an uninteresting activity. *Motivation and Emotion*, 26, 3, 186-207.

Reeve, J. (2009). Why teachers adopt a controlling motivating style toward students and how they can become more autonomy supportive. *Educational Psychologist*, 44, 159-175.

References

Reeve, J. (2006). Teachers as facilitators: What autonomy-supportive teachers do and why their students benefit. *The Elementary School Journal,* 106, 225-236.

Reeve, J., & Halusic, M. (2009). How K-12 teachers can put self-determination theory principles into practice. *Theory and Research in Education,* 7, 145-154. doi 10.1177/1477878509104319.

Reeve, J., Jang, H., Carrell, D., Jeon, S., & Barch, J. (2004). Enhancing students' engagement by increasing teachers' autonomy support. *Motivation and Emotion,* 28, 147-169.

Ryan, R.M. & Huta, V, & Deci, E.L. (2008). Living well: A self-determination theory perspective on eudaimonia. *Journal of Happiness Studies,* 9, 139-170.

Ryan, R.M. & Deci, E.L. (2000a). Intrinsic and extrinsic motivations: Classic definitions and new directions. *Contemporary Educational Psychology,* 25, 54-67.

Ryan, R.M. & Deci, E.L. (2000b). Self-determination theory and the facilitation of intrinsic motivation, social development, and well-being. *American Psychologist,* 55, 68-78.

Ryan, R.M. & Powelson, C. (1991) Autonomy and relatedness as fundamental to motivation and education. *Journal of Experimental Education,* 60, 49-66

Ryan, R.M., Huta, V. & Deci, E.L. (2008) Living well: A self-determination theory perspective on eudaimonia. *Journal of Happiness Studies,* 9. 139-170.

Ryff, C.D. (1989) Happiness is everything, or is it? Explorations on the Meaning of Psychological Well-Being. *Journal of Personality and Social Psychology,* 57, 6, 1069-1081.

Ryff, C.D. & Keyes, C.L.M. (1995). The structure of psychological well-being revisited. *Journal of Personality and Social Psychology,* 69, 4, 719-727.

Stephens, J.M. & Wangaard, D.B. (2011). *Creating a culture of academic integrity: A toolkit for secondary schools.* Minneapolis, MN: Search Institute.

Streight, D. (2015). *Breaking into the heart of character: Self-determined moral action and academic motivation*. Third edition. Portland, OR: CSEE.

Vansteenkiste, M., Sierens, E., Goossens, L., Soenens, B, Dochy, F., Mouratidis, A., Aelterman, N,, Haerens, L., & Byers, W. (2012). Identifying configurations of perceived teacher autonomy support and structure: Associations with self-regulated learning, motivation, and problem behavior. *Learning and Instruction*, 22, 431-439.

Warneken, F. & Tomasello, M. (2008). Extrinsic rewards undermine altruistic tendencies in 20-month-olds. *Developmental Psychology*, 44, 1785-1788.

Waterman, A.S. (1990). The relevance of Aristotle's conception of eudaimonia for the psychological study of happiness. *Theoretical and Philosophical Psychology*, 10, 1, 39-44.

Watson, M. & Ecken, L. (2003). *Learning to trust: Transforming difficult elementary classrooms through developmental discipline*. New York: John Wiley & Sons, Inc.

Weinstein, N. & Ryan, R.M. (2010). When helping helps: Autonomous motivation for prosocial behavior and its influence on well-being for the helper and recipient. *Journal of Personality and Social Psychology*, 98, 222-244. DOI: 10.1037/a0016984

Weissberg, R., Goren, P., Domitrovich, C. & Dusenbury, L. (2013) Effective social and emotional learning programs: Preschool and elementary school edition. Chicago, IL: Collaborative for Academic, Social, and Emotional Learning.

Thank you

I am indebted to a few colleagues who helped this book come together, and begin with John Roberts, who because of distance got to read less of it than of its predecessor, but whose editorial comments from that work have haunted the entirety of this one, for the better.

To Amanda Leaman, for most of the illustrations here, the more professional looking ones. I am also indebted to Amanda, on the eve of her departure from CSEE, for three years of seeing how we could do so many things better in the office, and then doing most of them; and for lovely detail and spirit in all the rest of her collaboration with us.

To Pamela Vohnson and Jenny Aanderud, both of whom found elusive errors, made embarrassment-precluding corrections, and offered valuable editorial comments before this manuscript went off to be printed. Jenny also designed the cover and assisted in a mountain of other ways.

And to Jillianne Bandstra, who probably is unaware of her contribution to the book, but whose enthusiasm for well-being at an early stage of the manuscript's development influenced the concept's deeper weave into some chapters, and thus made the entire work better.

And finally, to paraphrase a thank you at the end of *Breaking into the Heart of Character*, I am indebted to Edward Deci, Richard Ryan, and their many colleagues who have worked to understand, and to share with us, the power that volition and value, warmth and support, self-efficacy and competence have to help students flourish.

About the author

David Streight spent three decades either teaching or working as a school psychologist in a variety of schools. In addition to his book on modern Provençal poetry, *Théodore Aubanel: Sensual Poetry and the Provençal Church* (1994), he has translated a half-dozen books, primarily on Islam, for academic presses, and has edited or contributed to a half-dozen other books related to the fields of character development and fostering goodness in young people. The most recent of these is *Breaking into the Heart of Character*, of which this book is published as a "prequel." For the past eleven years he has been Executive Director of the Center for Spiritual and Ethical Education, in Portland, Oregon.